A Guide to Liberation Theology
for Middle-Class Congregations

A Guide to Liberation Theology
for Middle-Class Congregations

by

Charles H. Bayer

Wipf & Stock
PUBLISHERS
Eugene, Oregon

Except where indicated, scripture quotations are from the Revised Standard Version of the Bible, copyrighted 1946, 1952, © 1971, 1973 by the Division of Christian Education of the National Council of the Churches of Christ in the United States of America, and used by permission.

Wipf and Stock Publishers
199 W 8th Ave, Suite 3
Eugene, OR 97401

A Guide to Liberation Theology for Middle-Class Congregations
By Bayer, Charles H.
Copyright©1986 by Bayer, Charles H.
ISBN 13: 978-1-59244-903-3
ISBN 10: 1-59244-903-4
Publication date 3/19/2007
Previously published by CBP Press, 1986

Contents

	page
Preface	6
Introduction	10
1. The Captivity of the Oppressors	15
2. Liberation's Saving Gifts	24
3. The Recovery of Evangelism	40
4. The Liberation of Persons	52
5. Ideological Issues and Biblical Faith	68
6. Liberation Theology and Political Action	85
7. The Question of Violence	102
8. The Oppressed Too Close to See	120
9. Congregational Praxis	130
10. The Liberating Power of Passion	152
11. God's Final Victory	166

Preface

Of the writing of books about liberation theology there is no end. Most of this massive body of literature has taken one of three forms.

1. The seminal work of theologians, who show the power of God and the meaning of the Bible through the eyes of the marginalized and the poor, whose despair and hopes are the roots from which liberation theology has sprung. This category includes materials from feminist and black theologians, as well as the more familiar Third World authors.

2. Descriptions of the plight of the oppressed and the history of their oppression, usually produced by First World authors, whose compassion for the world's victims, identification with their suffering and anger at the complicity of the affluent are laid on our doorsteps.

3. Academic and scholarly studies of First World authors, who analyze and interpret the work of Third World theologians, and who define ways in which liberation theology is both similar to and different from traditional theological disciplines.

To this date, however, little has been written from the perspective of congregations in the First World, where many of us live and work. We in the middle-class, mainline churches are in the anomalous position of feeling guilty about the deplorable conditions our lifestyles and political attachments perpetuate for hundreds of millions of others, a perfectly appropriate locus of guilt, but whose own captivities are not addressed. Unless the liberation promised by God is also for us, the gospel is not a universal declaration of hope. Certainly liberation theology is fundamentally of, by, and for the poor. But it is my contention that the same biblical materials, the same hermeneutic and the same promise of liberation are also appropriate declarations of the gospel for the rest of us. This book has been prepared to help fill that void.

Many of us, clergy and laity, have read about liberation theology, have known the sting of its accusations, yet have felt powerless to respond in any way which alters either the conditions of the marginalized or our own. Others within our congregations have ducked the issues by assuming that the liberation enterprise is either Marxist, violent or both. That is, after all, what one is drawn to conclude when the popular press provides the basic curriculum.

Many others, having heard about the dim view the Vatican takes of liberationists, assume we are confronted by nothing more than an anti-Christian political movement dressed in religious garb. Resolutions condemning liberation theology have begun to show up in the ecclesiastical assemblies of First World churches. The National and World Councils of Churches, which are seen as generally in support of liberationism, have again been beaten about the head and shoulders by those who "know" that these inter-church agencies are somehow subservient to international forces abhorrent to the "free world."

This book takes quite a different perspective. It addresses those captivities peculiar to our middle-class, mainline, First World congregations and their members. It is not a how-to-do-it handbook, nor "ten easy steps to make your congregation a liberation church." Rather, it is a guide to understanding liberation thought and its implications for the unpoor. It argues that our captivities are directly tied to the desperate conditions of the marginalized, both those in the Third World and those in our midst. Few of us feel particularly oppressed. Yet there is the haunting feeling that neither are we free. We are caught in an oppressive matrix over which we have little control. The same gospel, which is liberating news for the poor, must somehow be liberating news for us as well.

I have sought to address the ordinary functions of our congregations: worship, preaching, pastoral counseling, weddings and funerals, healing, Bible study, education, social welfare, political action, world outreach, community service, stewardship, church growth and evangelism. If I were to select this book's one overarching theme it would be evangelism: the proclamation of the good news of the saving wholeness offered in Jesus Christ.

The author is a pastor, deeply committed to the work of the congregation. After two decades in parish ministry, the last seven years at an exciting university church in Chicago, I left the parish, believing I could more readily find the project God had given me to do from within secular culture. After three years as the chief executive officer of a not-for-profit corporation, I realized the congregation was, in fact, the basic instrument for acting out the freedom offered through the life and passion of Christ. If the signs of the kingdom were to be manifest, the congregation, with all its warts, was the most available vehicle for God to use. I returned to the pastorate and have served a middle-U.S., middle-class, mainline church since 1976.

The more I have been confronted by liberationism, the more deeply I have become convinced that even if it is primarily addressed to the poor, it is also addressed to us. The biblical account, which is the taproot of all liberation thought, has universal application. In the archetypal story of the Exodus, if we are not the slaves we must either be the Egyptians or those who keep Pharaoh in power. Yet in a way which transcends that too simple analogy, we are also among the unfree; captives of a destructive system which holds us in bondage to the principalities and powers of this world. We live in a double bondage: first, the bondage which strangles the oppressors in an oppressive system; second, the bondage which devolves from lives overburdened with material possessions and undernourished with the power and passion of the Spirit. Our prison bars are covered with dull, gray velvet.

Liberationism is not really a new theology. It is only a retelling of the biblical story of salvation and hope. It begins with the account of human bondage to sin and the consequences of sin, and ends with God's final victory and the coming of the kingdom.

As we sit at the feet of the wretched of the earth, we discover that their freedom is our hope. Both they and we are called to perform the special projects God has given us, using the particular gifts and graces God has assigned. Both they and we wait expectantly, even while we work, for that time when the kingdom of God will be established and God will reign forever and ever.

So many people have been part of this work. My thanks first of all to the congregation and staff of the First Christian Church in St. Joseph, Missouri, for both the time to complete the work and much of the raw materials which defined for me how a liberated congregation functions. Wally Reed, my associate in ministry, has been instrumental all the way along. Wendy, my wife, kept telling me I could do it, even when my doubts soared. Particular thanks must go to Dr. Martin Cressey and the Senatus of Westminister College, Cambridge, England, for their hospitality and encouragement. A special thanks is due my friend, Dr. Phil Mullins, who insisted I get a word processor during a period in my life when I sneered at all things technological. He was right, and I was wrong!

Charles H. Bayer
Cambridge, England 1985

Introduction

Liberation theology is an important contemporary discipline for all Christians, not only those in the Third World. It is not just about "them," meaning the poor. Neither is it a quixotic new theology; just one more in a series of theological fads. It is not even really a theology; it is *theology*. It is consistent with the essential message inherent in Christian teaching, although not always rendered explicit by traditional theological methodologies. Its major scriptural models—The Exodus, Jesus' mission announced in Nazareth, the parable of the last judgment—are universally applicable biblical paradigms.

Liberation theology focuses on God's salvific activities described in the biblical witness and beyond it. Liberation theology is not primarily concerned with economics or political ideologies, with philosophic notions of coherence or with the analysis of literary or anthropological data. Nor is it fundamentally concerned with propositional statements by which the faith has historically been articulated—that is, doctrine. Because these concerns have dominated the theological enterprise in North America and Europe, liberation theology does not appear to be in the mainstream. If, however, God is finally known through what God has done and is doing, then all the theoretical and systematic aspects of theology are only proximate descriptions of the divine/human encounter.

Liberation theology proposes that the church has been assigned specific projects to be realized in history. When I first encountered the word *project*, I was mildly unimpressed. A project is something I do in my basement on Saturday afternoon, or an article I get to when I have time. But liberationists use the term in quite a different way. It refers to the central evangelistic mission the church is called to perform within a particular historic, political and economic context. The doing of the project is not to be confused with the old liberal notion of bringing in God's kingdom. Liberation theology is not triumphalistic. The project is a halfway house, a roadside hostel on the way to the kingdom. It is what we do in celebration of the Messianic age Jesus introduced into human history. Our project involves acknowledging the birth of a more just social order. The final reign of God will be established without our aid, or permission. Praxis, or doing the truth, is the way by which the church comes to know God. Orthopraxis replaces orthodoxy, doing replaces reflection, as the fundamental theological mode.

The Bible, which is a record of God's redeeming activity, provides the basic design for the church's praxis. The specific nature of our project, however, flows from our historical particularities. One does not begin with either the Bible or doctrine in order to discover what to do and what to believe. God's acts always precede any record of them. The Bible describes what God has done. It also contains the orders we open as we embark on our mission.

Action first, God's liberating work, then the word. The interpretation of the biblical message is derived from one's own circumstances in light of God's liberating mandate. Liberationism overlays the biblical account with the conviction that God always stands alongside the oppressed, always is ready to free the marginalized, always challenges the principalities and powers which throttle and degrade human existence. Indeed, God has already disarmed these demonic forces. Our project entails giving evidence to what God has done. The theological flow is thus fourfold:

1. God's acts.
2. The record of God's acts, the Bible.
3. A hermeneutic which sees God as liberator within specific economic and social systems.
4. The performance by the church of the project assigned to it.

The book takes this four-fold pattern and applies it to the life and work of middle-class parishes in the First World. If the theologians of liberation are correct, and all theology must be done on location, then we must do it from where we stand, not from the perspective of a Peruvian village.

A liberating theology for the oppressors may be as important in the contemporary world as a liberating theology for the oppressed. Our captivity to the principalities and powers is dehumanizing. We suffer from it both collectively and as individuals. This book addresses that captivity and speaks about our liberation, as well as the liberation of the marginalized. Throughout we will operate from the perspective of the middle-class parish, focusing on the life and work of the congregation. From that vantage point we will deal with our own peculiar captivities, and attempt to define what the liberation of the oppressed means for us, as well as for the poor.

Chapter 1 sets the context by describing the captivity of the oppressors. Both the prisoners and the jailers live behind bars. We view Third World liberationism from the perspective of the Egyptians, not the Hebrews.

Chapter 2 discusses the gifts we have received from liberation theologians and from the basic communities out of which liberation theology springs. We will also see how these gifts impact the life and work of our congregations.

Chapter 3 defines evangelism in the congregation as the declaration, in action, of the liberating work of God in Jesus Christ; and sets off authentic evangelism from its trivializing manifestation, "church growth."

Chapter 4 addresses the particular captivities in which middle-class people find ourselves: the burden of the baggage we drag about with us, the boredom which has become a cultural epidemic, the prophylactic lives so many of us live.

Chapter 5 takes, head on, the major ideological problems which have prohibited many First World people from hearing what liberationists have to say. We discuss specifically: Marxism and spirituality. This chapter also lays out a biblical hermeneutic, which if used in congregations may help free the parish to become committed to a liberating praxis which is germane to its ongoing life and consistent with its nature.

Chapter 6 addresses how, and under what terms, congregations become involved in direct political action, a central element in the project God has assigned us.

Chapter 7 discusses the problem of violence, both in terms of the revolution of the poor and the institutionalized violence of the developed world, and links the twin themes of justice and peace.

Chapter 8 describes the meaning of liberation among two non-Third World groups: blacks and women.

Chapter 9 deals with models of congregational praxis, giving specific attention to the captivities which are peculiar to individuals in the developed world.

Chapter 10 continues to discuss the life and work of the congregation, and argues for a recovery of passion, both as the way compassion is concretized, and as a way out of the captivities of materialism, boredom and the prophylactic life.

Chapter 11 sets liberation theology in an eschatological framework.

Not only is the book written from the perspective of the middle-class congregation, its author may be hopelessly bourgeois. I do not pretend that the church I know and the life I lead are trapped in grinding poverty and despair. The major drafting was done in Westminister College, Cambridge, not in the barrios of Latin America. The audiences to whom it is addressed are not the oppressed of the Third World, but the unfree of the First World. As I was leaving my parish for four months in order to complete this work, a colleague remarked that going to Cambridge to write about liberation theology was like going to a five star restaurant to write about world hunger. But I am not writing about the oppression of the destitute, but about the captivities of the middle class. Without sidestepping the issues or dulling our agony about the wretched of the earth, this book seeks to be a faithful proclamation of the good news which is God's universal gift of grace.

This book is dedicated to the memory and liberated spirit of my son, John Mark Bayer, a young man of compassion and passion, who for me even in death remains a sign of God's kingdom.
"Home is the sailor, home from sea."

1

The Captivity of the Oppressors

Liberation theology is first of all about the oppressed. It views the Christian faith through the eyes of the poor, the wretched of the earth, the non-person. It proclaims God's solidarity with the left out and the destitute, the ratted on and spat upon.

Since Gustavo Gutierrez defined it more than two decades ago, the influence and power of liberation theology have been dominant forces in Christian thought in the world of the oppressors and the oppressed. Scores of books have been directed both to the poor and the unpoor. The poor have been called to receive God's liberating work as their own, and the unpoor to solidarity with them. All who have given serious thought to the implications of the gospel are indebted to those who have introduced us to the work and will of God seen through the eyes of the world's destitute.

Most of us in the "developed world" who read these books are not destitute. I do not feel oppressed. I am the senior minister of a solid middle-class congregation in the heartland of the United States, where the research for this book was substantially done. The manuscript was drafted on a sophisticated computer in the comfortable confines of Cambridge, England. It is addressed not to the wretched of the earth, but to the affluent, those who make up most mainline Protestant and Catholic congregations and judicatories in the developed world. I doubt if many of you reading these pages have no food for tomorrow. I doubt if your children have no schools, no medical treatment and no hope. You will not be sleeping on the streets. Many of you receive incomes every week in excess of what the poor of the world earn in a year.

One of the tasks of liberation theology is to sensitize us to the plight of our brothers and sisters who are hungry, cold and wretched. It is assumed that knowing about them will somehow change our attitudes, and a change in attitude, it is hoped, will change our action. Yet that perspective flies in the face of what liberation theology is all about. It is initially concerned with action, not attitudes. It is not overly fascinated with how you interpret the Bible; what the scholarly evidence is for believing this doctrine or that. It is first of all concerned with doing the truth, not understanding it or even believing it. It begins with God's saving action and continues in the action of God's people. Liberation theology is about orthopraxis—right action—not orthodoxy—right belief, or more accurately, right praise.

Liberation theology calls the affluent of the world not only to stand in solidarity with the poor and the oppressed, but ultimately to become like Christ the Lord, who "for your [our] sake he became poor, so that by his poverty you [we] might become rich" (2 Corinthians 8:9). The chances are modest at best, however, that many who read this or any other book on the subject will renounce their wealth and privilege and join the poor in their plight. Our level of charity might be increased, and that would be a blessing in itself, but the likelihood is that most of us will end up in the same comfortable posture in relation to the wretched of the earth that we took before we read a single line. Not many of us will sell all we have, give the proceeds to the poor and follow Jesus. We will be quick to point out that this was a command to a particular rich young man, not a universal imperative. This sidestep begins to define our captivity.

Obviously one need not go to Brazil to encounter poverty and oppression. These demonic forces are all around, as are the humiliation of racism, sexism and the other manifestations of the principalities and powers which disfigure the human family. Even in our own democratic and relatively free land, many suffer because of ruthless, unjust and inhuman systems which the affluent allow to continue. Most of us have made peace with these systems, knowing their demise would cause us inconvenience, if not massive economic dislocation. Yet, liberation theology is about much more than improving the lot of the marginalized in our midst, as valuable and godly a goal as that might be. It is rather about a new order in which God has chosen sides with the poor, and we are not poor!

It has been easy for many of us in the affluent world to rid ourselves of having to deal with liberation theology because of the political and economic philosophy to which it seems inextricably attached. "Oh, that's communistic, you know." Thus ends the discussion. For years the Vatican has been involved in a heated debate with liberation theologians about whether they, the liberationists, have traded the gospel for an economic theory. Not that the church, Protestant and Catholic, has historically refused to bed down with economic theories when it has been to its advantage. Most of the folk in our parishes seem quite comfortable with capitalism, and would be disquieted in the extreme if they were told that to mix it up with their religion was somehow scandalous.

For these and other reasons liberation theology has seemed, at best, a noble albeit alien perspective, which has to do with Latin Americans and other less fortunate people, but not with us. In fact, among the churches in the United States which are experiencing fresh bursts of popularity, liberation theology is more a despised heresy—along with humanism and liberalism—than even a curiosity. Enthusiasm for liberationism seems to be in inverse ratio to the capacity of a church to grow. In an era fascinated by church growth, liberation theology is held to be counter productive. It doesn't work! For those who deify pragmaism, what doesn't work is not only useless, it is downright dangerous.

If liberation theology is only relevant to the oppressed, why should those of us who are not oppressed bother with it? Is it to be reduced to an intellectual exercise, something to tickle our guilt, or make us feel more righteous than others if we can quote its axioms and properly pronounce the names of its major exponents? If so, it has become only another illustration of the intellectual dilettantism which all too often marks the theological discipline.

But what if it is much more than a curious aberration? What if it proclaims the gospel for us; reveals the God we have been unable to see because we have been blinded by our affluence? What if our salvation and the salvation of our society is at stake? Then we avoid what it says, or what God says through it, at our peril.

At another level liberation theology reminds us that all theology must be done from within a particular historical and cultural context. In Latin America the context is that of an oppressed majority living at the mercy of an affluent minority at home and a faceless tyranny abroad. But that is not our context. It is a major thesis of this book that while liberation theology provides an exciting articulation of the gospel among the poor, we miss the thrust of the message unless we see it from a vantage point which is distinctly ours. I believe liberation theology speaks directly to us and our situation. It is the revelation of God's word and truth confronting us in a way quite different from the way it confronts the wretched of the earth.

Consider the trilogy of paradigmatic texts most cited by liberation theologians: the Exodus, Jesus' declaration of his mission at Nazareth and the parable of the last judgment. If they seem first of all directed to the poor, the coin has another side. They also speak to us about our situation and its consequences.

In the Exodus account there is no neutral ground. No Egyptian family is spared, because every Egyptian family is part of the oppressive system. Jesus' homily, following his reading from Isaiah 61 at his home synagogue, scandalized his hearers when he described God's commitment to outsiders. In the parable of the last judgment, the excuse offered by the affluent that they didn't realize it was Jesus they neglected, doesn't work.

These are but three of the hundreds of biblical allusions which form the intellectual and thematic heart of liberation thought. In the struggle between the oppressed and the oppressors, God stands with the oppressed. God has taken up their cause. God is their liberator. God has a preferential option for the poor. God's role in history is to free them from their oppression; and through them, all creation. Liberation illumines the exchatological meaning of history—"to reconcile to himself all things, whether on earth or in heaven"(Colossians 1:20).

Those who are not the oppressed are the oppressors, and the oppressors are neither free nor whole. Indeed, the oppressors suffer from an intolerable bondage just as do the oppressed. Both are trapped by sin and its consequences. Pharaoh is not even free to do the right thing. He is so caught up in the system that his heart is hardened and he cannot let the people go.

Dorothee Soelle suggests that if in today's world the poor and the oppressed are the Hebrews, then we, if not actually the Egyptians, have acclimated ourselves to a manner of life with which Egyptians are very comfortable.

> The real exile of Christians in the First World is that we have learned to endure it. We have adjusted ourselves so much to Egypt that we feel at home. We have adjusted ourselves to the Egyptian lifestyle. We have adopted the basic beliefs of the Egyptians. . . . We have learned to endure the exile so well that we no longer see ourselves as exiled people—as strangers in a strange land. Quite the contrary, we attempt to Egyptize the whole world . . . We see no need for liberation.[1]

The distastefulness of that allegation is obvious. No one likes to think of him/herself as an oppressor. Most of the people I know do not fit the Egyptian mold. We are, on the whole, a good people; a kindly, charitable, generous people. We do what we can to alleviate the suffering in the world. As William McElveney says:

> We go about our daily work, raise our families, support the church and/or various civic organizations that reach out to human need, enjoy a few friends and live out our lives. So what's so oppressive about that?[2]

His book, *Good News Is Bad News Is Good News*, reinforces Soelle's inference. We are so caught up in our own cultural systems that we have failed to realize we are, in fact, the Egyptians.

Yet in a prison—or in an oppressive society—the jailer is just as much behind bars as the jailed. Was Pharoah so enmeshed in his own oppressive world he could not change his mind even if he had wanted to? Are we so conditioned by our oppressiveness that we are hopelessly trapped, lost and condemned to live and die in it?

McElvaney believes there is hope "Pharaoh" might see the light. In fact, he insists that if Pharaoh only wakes up and discovers the value of the rights of others, he too will be set free from his own unrecognized slavery. Given human nature, that may be asking a bit much of Pharaoh. Only by grace does Pharaoh's conversion appear remotely possible. Oppressive systems which seem to work for the good of a few are not that easily given up by those on top.

Yet it is the system which traps us, and be we oppressed or oppressors, we are all ensnarled in its sticky web. We are all controlled by what St. Paul called, "The principalities and powers of this present age." When, because of sin, there is no freedom for the oppressed, neither can there be freedom for the oppressor. That is the nature of sin; its consequences are universal. Something about that argument, however, seems to relieve the pressure, allows us to protest, "who me?" and provides a handy legitimization for failing to alter our action.

Nor does the oppressor suffer the same day by day deprivations as the oppressed. I may be a jailer, and I may be behind the same bars as the jailed, but I get to go home every evening. I do not eat in the prison cafeteria. I can travel where I want and do what I want—within reason. The jailed cannot. In fact, the knowledge that the conditions of the jailed and the conditions of the jailer are radically different is comforting. Is it not a matter of considerable boasting that people in the United States are the most affluent in the world; perhaps in the history of the world? I don't run across many folks in our congregations, judicatories, denominational headquarters, agencies, seminaries or publishing companies eager to change the system. We may be willing to fine tune it, but we would be horrified, most of us, at the thought of revolution. So when ominous revolutionary sounds are heard in Latin America, we quickly dismiss them as the indigestive rumblings of a Soviet plot.

THE CAPTIVITY OF THE OPPRESSORS   21

When you got your last raise, bought your last car, refrigerator, microwave, word processor or VCR, did you complain about the injustice which stalks the world? My guess is that we rather enjoy our opulence. Even in our churches we seldom allude to the problem, except in the proper liturgical form of our solemn assemblies, where we may even receive "an offering for the poor." And, if Amos showed up there, he would probably be less welcome than he was when he commented on conditions in Bethel.

In the heart of the Bible-loving, antebellum South it would have been a scandal to suggest that the slave owners were just as much in captivity as the slaves. Certainly what went on in that society was not considered a matter of religion. Religion was about heaven, not about slavery.

Whether the allegation that we are the Egyptians is an accurate analogy is beside the point. Even if it is exactly the truth, the whole truth and nothing but the truth, hearing it and even believing it will not, and indeed has not, altered our actions very much. I may suffer from a twinge of guilt now and then. Yet when breakfast time rolls around I have no particular qualms about downing, at miraculously cheap prices, my coffee and banana-covered corn flakes, both laced with sugar. It does not occur to me that three of the four items on the menu come as a direct result of the exploitation of the Hebrews by the Egyptians; and my breakfast identifes me as the latter. Nor is it a matter of intellectual dullness. All of us remotely familiar with the literature realize that exploitation involves the substitution of cash crops for food crops. The rich get richer, the poor get poorer. But I enjoy my breakfast, the world goes on, and the noise of our solemn assemblies is amplified by the marvels of electronic gadgetry.

Liberation theology informs us that while I linger over a second cup of coffee, God is getting ready to turn the Nile—or the Caribbean—red with blood. It has not been that long ago the first-born sons in a great many U.S. homes were killed. The angel of death stopped by Egypt on his way to Vietnam, where he had other business to conduct.

If in the Exodus story there is little if any sympathy for the Egyptians, the Christian affirmation offers another dimension.

The gospel declares that God loves and wills to redeem the whole creation, and that includes us. If Pharaoh seemed to be outside the providence of God, we are not. Indeed, in the long run—which is another way of saying God's own time—all things will be redeemed. Thus the Christian hope is both in history and in God's plan for last things.

Instead of thinking of the problem in terms of the oppressed and the oppressors, even though I believe it to be a demonstrable reality, it might be more conducive to action, to praxis, if we understand that both we and our oppressed brothers and sisters are part of God's single plan to unite all things in Godself, things in heaven and things on earth. For now we share the occupancy of this fallen creation; all of us living in hope that the world will be set free from its bondage to sin and to death and inherit the glorious liberty of the children of God. Our redemption has been begun in Christ. We are invited, indeed we are commissioned, to participate in its flowering through our project which points to an ultimate reality. We return to the eschatological dimension in the final chapter. For now, our question has to do with the redemption of the oppressors in history, not beyond it.

As Henri Nouwen says: "Jesus the Lord, loves the oppressor as well as the oppressed and entered into history to set all men and women free."[3] Gutierrez puts it this way: "Liberation is an all-embracing process that leaves no dimension of human life untouched, because when all is said and done it expresses the saving action of God in history."[4]

Even if most of us who live in middle-class comfort do not feel oppressed, just as we do not consider ourselves as particularly oppressive, in the light of the gospel we are not free, nor do we live in a free world. Being part of an unfree world we stand in need of liberation which is a gift and promise of God. Hence, liberation theology speaks a word of hope to us and our situation. We too share the degradation of the sinfulness which has produced oppression. We too are subject to the futility and death which stalks the creation. We too groan in travail with the creation as it struggles to be set free. We too stand in need of hearing, receiving and celebrating the liberating gospel. The good news is not just for the wretched of the earth—although it first comes to them and we receive it by their graciousness and God's—it is also for us. Not to escape the harsh reality, or crawl out from under the conviction of our sinfulness, but as a way to look at the problem which may be more conducive to action, we will throughout this study see ourselves as captives, as well as oppressors.

Liberation theology is primarily about evangelism. Not the pseudo-evangelism which has been popularized in the church growth movement, but the declaration of the evangel; the good news that God has acted in Christ to redeem the creation. With the rest of the natural order we stand on tiptoes, eager to see the children of God coming into their own.

Ours, however, is not a passive waiting. We have already heard the good news, and have been called, according to God's purpose, to share in the project of the kingdom. So this book belongs on the shelves of your church library under the category: evangelism. It is addressed to us, the half-saved, the still unliberated citizens of this world, who struggle and pray so we might enter God' kingdom.

Robert McAfee Brown quotes Dom Helder Camera as saying to a visiting group of North Americans:

> If you are appalled by what you see here, please don't try to start a revolution for us—a revolution from which you can flee when real bullets start flying. If you really want to help us, go back to your own country and work to change the policies of your government that exploit our country and keep our people so poor.[5]

To engage in liberating praxis is to proclaim the gospel; the good news that we can be set free. We need live no longer drugged by opiates served up by the principalities and powers. We can be part of God's liberating action. That is what evangelism in the congregation, and beyond, really means.

Notes

1. Dorothee Soelle, *The Challenge of Liberation Theology*, ed. by Brian Mahan and Dale L. Richeson. Orbis, 1984. p. 5.
2. William McElveney, *Good News Is Bad News Is Good News*. Orbis, 1981. p. 43.
3. Gustavo Gutierrez, *We Drink from Our Own Wells*. Orbis, 1984. p. xvii.
4. *Ibid.* p. 2.
5. Robert McAfee Brown, *Unexpected News*. Westminister, 1984. p. 44.

2

Liberation's Saving Gifts

Nothing has deadened our capacity to hear, appreciate and use the insights of liberation theology more than the accusation it is socialism dressed up in theological garb. While it is true that socialism has been one of the basic tools by which many Latin American, and other Third World apologists, have interpreted the liberation theme, its insights and actions range far beyond any social or political hermeneutic.

Although we will examine the relationship between liberationism and Marxism at great length in chapter five, it is exterior to the purpose of this book to debate the relative merits or demerits of economic theories. Using the same biblical and historical materials, one can make a case for and against both socialism and capitalism, depending on the cultural background against which the analysis is made. That is why theology must always be done on location. What is true in Wichita, Kansas, may not be true in Lima, Peru. It is not the gospel which changes from place to place, only the usefulness of any particular way of understanding it. A different kit of cultural data and interpretive tools produces a different set of conclusions. Societal idioms defy specific translation just as do linguistic ones.

What is clear to anyone who has looked carefully at the record, however, is that free enterprise as practiced in the developed world may have enriched the few in Third World nations, but their prosperity has usually been at the expense of the many.

At the root of the social unrest in Latin America is a class struggle. This does not exist because Marx identified it; he only named it. Call it what you may, when there is a tiny oligarchy of wealthy families, who hold power by violence, international alliances and fear; and a large body of landless and helpless peasants, who are tired of living on the brink of despair, and have discovered they no longer need to do so, class struggle is what you get.

If we are to be set free from our captivity—from sin and the consequences of sin—we must sit at the feet of our brothers and sisters in the Third World, the poor to whom the gospel has been given, and learn from them. They have much to teach us and many gifts to offer. But first we must lay aside labels which reduce the discussion to an ideological competition between capitalism and communism.

That is not to say we idealize the poor. We do not learn from them because they are more righteous than others. Gustavo Gutierrez reminds us that the world of the poor is made up of:

> flesh and blood human beings, pervaded with the forces of life and death, grace and sin. In that world we find indifference to others, individualism, abandoned children, people abusing people, pettiness, hearts closed to the action of the Lord.[1]

Nevertheless, the illusion that we have all the answers to the issues before the world and have nothing to learn from the poor, is part of our captivity. A prerequisite to our salvation is learning to sit quietly and hear the testimony of the marginalized. How else can we transcend the narrow limitations of our own perspectives?

I first discovered how much I had to learn from the poor in 1965. I was in the Caribbean with a group of U.S. Christians. We were examining revolutions and their impact on the church. We had been to Mexico and had observed the somber results of a burned-out revolution. Four of us were able to enter the Dominican Republic the day after the 82nd Airborne arrived, and had witnessed a revolution in progress. Our government had purportedly sent troops to secure the blessings of freedom to these benighted people. What we discovered was that we had intervened in the internal affairs of a sovereign nation because it had become increasingly clear that in an upcoming election the party less friendly to corporate interests in the United States might win. But that is another story.

Most of our time was spent in the poverty-stricken nation of Haiti, where we were investigating a revolution that had not yet occurred. Perhaps there are some places so desperate that there is not energy even for revolution. It was on the veranda of a hotel near Port-a-Prince where I was confronted by the Christ of the poor. We had spent the day in the city, observing the hope-deadening and life-draining effects of despair. But we were visitors. We were not there to share in the suffering, let alone relieve it; only to observe it.

After a tiring day of observation, we retreated to a suburban hotel reserved for foreigners, or anyone wealthy enough to enjoy its luxury. It was a relief to be away from the smell, filth and depravity of the city. One can only take so much poverty! It was while having dinner on the veranda of that hotel I was encountered by Christ.

The hotel hung like an eagle's eyrie on the side of a mountain a few miles above the city. It was a warm romantic night. The sea breeze, rising to meet the foothills, cooled us. Below stretched the twinkling tiny lights of homes, with their outdoor stoves. The sounds of drums could be heard in the distance. There were bells, far-off voices and the barking of dogs. Through the haze of the city I could see the harbor, where two cruise ships lay at anchor. The atmosphere was pure, idyllic, Caribbean magic.

Our dinner was graciously served as we sat lost in the "native charm" below us. Well, we had been down amidst that "charm" during the day, but anyone with a poetic imagination could escape the reality of what was there, and we did.

As I recall, the meal consisted of fine wine, a lovely salad of tropical fruits, a fish stuffed with crab meat and rice accompanied by an exotic sauce: a tropical feast! It was the kind of meal those below, who lived with the drums and the fires, had probably never even seen. We were protected from any unpleasantness by a heavy iron fence which surrounded the hotel's sizeable lawn.

As I was luxuriating in the elegance of that meal, suddenly

before me stood a woman holding an emaciated child in her stick-thin arms. She was so gaunt that she had been able to slip through the bars of the fence. She was but one of perhaps a hundred mothers with dying children near the gates of our hotel. But we had seen enough of that during the day, and had been walled in to escape the rigors of having to confront any more human despair.

This woman had crawled in the shadows around the perimeter of the lawn and had made it to the edge of the veranda, where she stood before me with her pitiful child. I was shocked, not so much at the intrusion, but by the despair on her face. Slowly she raised her arms, holding her child out to me. There were no words, but from her eyes came the message, "My child is starving."

What could I do? I was immobilized, helpless. As I was about to hand her my half-eaten plate of food, the manager of the hotel abruptly appeared accompanied by two armed guards, who seized the woman and her child, and hustled them away to join the others lost in the shadows beyond our view. In a few moments, the sweating embarrassed host returned to my table overcome with the humiliation of what had just happened. "I'm so very sorry," he said. "I hope she did not spoil your dinner."

He did not know how many dinners of mine that woman would spoil for the next twenty years. Someday I will stand before the Lord of history, who will separate the nations as a shepherd separates the sheep from the goats. And he will say to me, and the the citizens of my society, "I was hungry and you did not feed me; thirsty and you gave me nothing to drink; naked, homeless, a stranger and you did not minister to me." The image of that mother and the thousands of others I saw that day will flash across my mind. Mothers and their babies still starve in Haiti a quarter of a century later. I still have not ministered to the Christ who continues to appear to me through them. Even now I do not know how to escape that captivity.

Perhaps the most important gift we have to receive from the wretched of the earth is the living presence of the Lord. If so, and if that presence finally reorders our lives, we may too be liberated from sin and its consequences. As we learn from the poor and from those who have articulated the gospel of liberation on their behalf, other saving gifts are offered. Liberation theology can save us from certain deeply rooted illusions which we, the non-poor, have long cherished. That gift may not only change our opinions by providing new information and insights, but of much more significance, our actions may also be dramatically altered.

Consider just one of the comfortable myths by which we live, both as citizens and as members of First World churches, the myth that somehow the plight of the wretched of the earth can be alleviated through the investment of U.S. capital and the accompanying economic development our capital generates. It has always made sense for us to divide the world into two parts: the developed world and the underdeveloped world. We live in one. *They* live in the other. If underdevelopment is the problem, then development would seem to be the solution.

Pursuant to that obvious theory we have, in the developed world, spent enormous amounts of money in the belief that we would be able to replicate our gentler world among the impoverished masses. We build plants, provide employment, organize an infrastructure and deploy teams of specialists to the end that underdeveloped nations might enjoy the economic benefits we take for granted. What could be more fitting for a benevolent people to do, or more Christlike?

It is therefore startling to hear from the poor, and those who articulate the gospel through and for them, that developmentalism in the Third World has not only failed to work, but has been part of the problem. While purporting to serve the interests of the poverty stricken, it has served the interests of the developers, and the oligarchy in the underdeveloped world, with whom the developers have made common cause. It has been a boon to the rich and a stone around the necks of the afflicted.

Gutierrez, speaking of the developers, puts it this way: "Not only have they failed to eliminate the prevailing economic system, they have contributed to its consolidation."[2] He continues:

> *Developmentalism* thus came to be synonymous with *reformism* and modernization, that is to say, synonymous with timid measures, really ineffective in the long run and counterproductive to achieving a real transformation. The poor countries are becoming ever

more clearly aware that their underdevelopment is only a by-product of the development of other countries, because of the kind of relationship which exists between the rich and the poor countries.³

The Brazilian theologian, Jose Miguez Bonino, holds that: "Development is a euphemism for neocolonialism, featuring cheap labor, raw materials and economic dependence."⁴

Or hear this judgment:

Development . . . promotes for the minority an increased income which enables them to become more closely integrated socially, culturally, ideologically and politically among themselves and into the world system, so conspicuously evident in their adoption of First World patterns of consumption. At the same time it promotes the impoverishment of the masses who are marginal to the system, a source of cost in a system that does not depend on their labor or their purchasing power.⁵

Developmentalism turns out to be another form of economic aggression. If overt colonialism has long since gone out of style, at least in the Western world, it now has reappeared in the guise of benevolence.

If we are to move from privilege and power to the generation of a preferential option for the poor, developmentalism seems to be a way further into the quagmire, not out of it. Wealthy landed oligarchies, the military establishments which have traditionally supported them and even sectors of the church—the third leg of the old despotic triad in Latin America—have benefited and continue to benefit from development. But the poor, the powerless, the landless, have been more and more isolated from hope and decency by developmental policies and practices.

If among liberationists one fails to hear a single kind word about it, we may question whether a blanket condemnation of developmentalism is appropriate. Evidence that it has been effective in lifting the burden of otherwise impoverished populations here and there in the Third World does exist. The problem may lie in the way developmentalists have gone about their tasks.

Some styles of aid to developing nations do meet the needs of vast numbers of the poor, and not just the greed of oligarchies and their hangers on. The accusations, however, hold enough truth to merit our attention and action. If in our congregations and other church bodies, we live with the myth that development automatically means salvation for the wretched of the earth, then our liberation may lie in hearing the truth from those who suffer from certain of its manifestations.

Our task is to reorder our action, our praxis, and that of the religious institutions in which we live, worship and work. Common sense, as well as commitment to the gospel, tells us that if we have been unwittingly supporting a destructive course of action, we are obliged to stop at the first available moment and reverse our direction. The religious words for this activity are *repentance* and *conversion*.

Here, as elsewhere, the active response of the church following its conversion, must necessarily be political. In the name of human decency our government, and the economic order it represents, has sold development as a way out for the wretched of the earth. If, in fact, our Latin American brothers and sisters are telling us the truth, and we have been co-opted by clever political ideologists, then we must seek political remedies. Remember the counsel of Dom Helder Camera—don't make a revolution for us. Go home and change your system which has throttled us and threatened our existence.

The church can no more divorce itself from politics than it can divorce itself from spiritual matters. To turn our backs on the political remedies essential in addressing economic problems is both sophistry and a recapitulation of the docetic heresy. It is to deny that Jesus came in the flesh. The response to those in our congregations and among our denominational leaders who insist the church has no business being involved in politics, is evangelism. As we shall see, to take the gospel seriously is to take politics seriously; more about that in chapter six.

Another saving gift we receive from the hands of the poor, concerns more directly the nature and work of parishes. New styles and shapes of local church life have arisen among the impoverished masses in Latin America. They suggest potential ways we can most effectively structure life and work within our congregations.

First, a definition of the church which comes from one of the most thoughtful of all Latin American theologians, Leonardo Boff. Although this definition describes "the Church," it holds true also for parishes and other local and regional manifestations of Christian life and work.

> The *Church* is that part of the world that, in the strength of the Spirit, has accepted the Kingdom made explicit in the person of Jesus Christ, the Son of God, incarnated in oppression. It preserves the constant memory and consciousness of the Kingdom, celebrating its presence in the world, shaping the way it is proclaimed and at the service of the world. The Church is not the Kingdom but rather a sign (explicit symbol) and its instrument (mediation) in the world.[6]

With that definition in mind, we might describe congregations as demonstration projects of the Kingdom; beachheads, precursors, evidences of what life will be like when God has become sovereign of all. Needless to say, that has not been the self-image of the church historically in Latin America, either among dominant Catholic populations or among the multitude of much smaller Protestant bodies. One wonders if many congregations where we work and worship hold any such self-understanding.

Boff cites other models of church, which previously dominated the life and thought of Latin American Christians, and I dare say of many north of the Mexican border as well. Two of these models concern us directly, for they reflect the way in which most modern parishes and other church related institutions, manifestations and agencies in the First World define themselves.

1. *The Church as the City of God:* The church is the exclusive bearer of salvation; meaning life in heaven. It offers that gift through its sacraments and liturgy. It is clergy-oriented and dominated. It avoids worldly matters, particularly politics, at all costs. It accommodates to the political realities with which it lives. Its

main task is to get folk ready for the next world, not to live abundant lives in this one.

2. *The Church as Mother and Teacher:* Although this seems a particularly Roman way to put it, many Protestants also see the church as a benevolent maternalistic enterprise. She instructs and cares for her children. She is sensitive to the physical needs of the poor. She establishes networks of social service programs. She encourages the upper classes to be caring and generous with the lower classes. She, however, makes a fine distinction between her religious charitable work and the structure and shape of society. Hers may be a church for the poor, but it is certainly not a church of the poor. They are only objects of her concern.[7]

In the 70s, however, there arose a new model, at least new to Latin American Catholics; and to most of the rest of us as well. This model is variously called: "the church of the poor," "the people's church," "basic Christian communities," or "base churches." Since this model holds ecclesiastical authority at arm's length, its proliferation has greatly disturbed the Vatican. The question it raises is more magisterial than theological: Who's in charge? In the all too rigid and moribund church life of many of our congregations, the development of these base communities may provide yet another gift. We are not poor, and therefore we cannot be the church of the poor. But we may here find clues to the revitalization of our congregational life and work.

Perhaps the simplest way to describe the genesis of these base communities, and what they do, is to tell a mythical, but not untrue, story of one of them. The outline was suggested in a sermon the the Rev. Kenneth Mahler, Lutheran Bishop of Panama, preached in the fall of 1984 at the First Lutheran Church of St. Joseph, Missouri. The setting could be many places in Latin America, but to give it a specific location we will set it in El Salvador.

The village of Nueva had never been prosperous. For many years its people had scraped a meager existence from the hilly land. Yet as inhospitable as was the countryside, they were able to provide for their needs by growing a bit of corn, beans and squash. Although most of the land was controlled by one clan, each peasant family had a tiny plot, as well as a job on the large farm the clan owned.

A few years back, things began to change. The elders of the clan moved to the city, and the land was leased to strangers the people of Nueva did not know. Gossip had it that whoever they were, they now controlled most of the land in the province. The shock was in the way the land was being used. No longer did it produce corn, beans and squash. It became part of a great banana plantation. All year machines, which had replaced the peasants who formerly worked the land, tended the trees and carted off the bananas to the seacoast where they were loaded on ships.

Life was all the more difficult for the people of Nueva. But what could they do? While they suffered, the clan in the city seemed to be doing very well. They bought and leased out more and more land. Even the small plots the peasants once cultivated were gone. When you need money to survive you will sell everything!

There was a church in the village, a lovely chapel built with the hands of the villagers many generations ago. But there were few masses and no priests. Occasionally a priest would come from the city to baptize their children, hear their confessions and perform their marriages; and then mass would be said. But for every service the priest performed there would be a charge. By the time the sun set the people were poorer and the priest much richer. But such was life. It had been that way for a long time; as long as the oldest man in Nueva could remember.

One day, quite unexpectedly, the bishop of the province arrived, and with him a young man dressed in jeans and an open shirt. "I have brought you a priest, who will be staying in your village," said the bishop. "He will work with you, and all the people in the countryside, for a year."

"He cannot be a priest," the people whispered to one another. "No priest ever stayed in our village. He is not even dressed like a priest. Perhaps he is a Protestant!"

The next day the bishop left, but the young man stayed. He said mass, married three couples and baptized their children.

When the holy services were over, the priest said to the people: "Tonight we will have a meeting. Juan, you have the largest house in the village, and that is where we will meet. I want you to see that every villager is present. It will be an important assembly."

No one would miss a meeting like that, and at sunset every adult in Nueva crowded into Juan's simple home. Juan had to put his modest furniture on the street to make room. When everyone had gotten into the house, the priest opened a large box he had brought with him. It was full of books, and one was given to each person.

"Tonight we will begin our life together by studying the Bible," said the priest. "Turn please to the first chapter of Exodus." There was an embarrassed silence. Only a few people in the village had seen a Bible before; the large one that was kept locked in the church. And even those who remembered seeing it had never heard of Exodus. The priest looked around. Some people were holding their Bibles upside down. Most sat quietly not knowing what to do. It was soon apparent no one in the village could read.

"The meeting is over for tonight," said the priest. "You cannot study the Bible if you cannot read. Beginning tomorrow night, and every night, we will meet in this home and we will learn to read and write. I will be here one week each month. I have three other villages as well as yours to care for."

The next night everyone was present again, and the first reading lesson was held. At the end of a year the priest again brought out the box he had opened his first day in Nueva. The people turned to Exodus and began to read. All that month they studied, when the priest was present and when he had gone to his other villages. They could not believe the stories they read! God had sent Moses to people who were without hope—slaves in Egypt—people who had no land and no money and no doctors and no schools. After a terrible struggle the people were set free.

"God loves you," said the priest. "You are God's favorite people, because you suffer the most. God wants to set you free from your oppression. God wants you to have your own land and your own crops. But you must want to be free just as much as did the people in Egypt."

As the weeks went by other stories were read. The people heard about Amos and Micah, and how God always befriended the victims, the downtrodden, people just like the villagers of Nueva. Later they read the most thrilling stories of all, the wonderful accounts about Jesus, who had said that his mission was to preach good news to the poor, free the captives, let the blind see, untie the ropes of the prisoners, and that the time for all of that to happen was right then. Jesus had come to the poor and he had brought with him a new way of living; he called it the kingdom of God.

Now the people of Nueva knew that Jesus had been sent into the world for them, for the simple people of their village. They were to be set free by the very same Jesus they had known about only when they received his body at mass. One day the priest said, "My good friends, I must leave you now. I shall only come back for a day every two months. But Jesus will not leave you. Now you have the stories, your stories, and you must work with Jesus who was poor just like you. He has given you a project to do. He will help you win your freedom."

It was not long thereafter that two of the wisest and bravest men of the village decided to go to the city and talk with the leaders of the province. If they were to be set free, as Jesus had promised, first of all they must have some of their land back. Surely not every acre was needed for bananas. They needed a doctor and a school and a voice in what happened to the money their village produced for the clan.

But when they arrived in the city they discovered that the politicians who ran the province were the same members of the clan, the very wealthy clan, from whom they formerly rented their little plots of ground.

"We have come to ask that some of our land be returned to us so we can grow food," the village leaders said. When they returned to Nueva it was not with land, it was with great welts on their backs where they had been beaten for their insolence. The next week they returned to the city to try again, taking three others with them. No one returned home for a week, and when they finally did they told of how life was in the jail with only stale crusts and water.

But the power of the stories in the book they had learned to read would not go away, and they knew God never made it easy for the slaves to be freed. There was another trip to the city. But this time the two wisest and strongest men of Nueva were shot. During the next months others were shot, and still there was no land, no freedom and no hope.

In time they made a remarkable discovery. Theirs was not the only church of the poor. All over the province groups of Christians were meeting in homes, just as they met—scores of little groups. Leaders from each of the villages began to gather and talk about ways they could work together for their freedom. Hope began to spread throughout the province, the kind of hope not even the guns used against them were able to extinguish.

Land and freedom have not yet come to the people of Nueva, but they have the stories now; they know that Jesus came to liberate them, and together with many others in the province, they will not rest until they are out of Egypt.

The basic community in Nueva is but one new style of congregational life developed in recent years. In urban areas the shape is somewhat different, although the general goals are much the same. Throughout Latin America thousands of these base communities have sprung up. In them we see Christ bringing "release to the captives." We may also find in these new styles of congregational life, serendipitous clues to the liberation of our more rigid and lifeless local institutions.

As freedom comes to the marginalized in the Nuevas of the Third World, a simultaneous gift comes to us. We are given the opportunity to be set free from our role as oppressors, or at least as those who keep the oppressors propped up. Without that burden, life for us may break out in ways so fraught with new potential that we will wonder why we spent decades bogged down in an oppressive system. Pharaoh was not free until the Hebrews were free. If the way freedom came was devastating to Pharaoh, at least he subsequently had the opportunity to make decisions he was unable even to consider as long as his energies were being consumed in keeping the oppressed in their places. As God is at work among the wretched of the earth, freeing them, the same dynamic may be freeing us from the captivities of the affluent, and we will examine this in later sections of the book.

An alternative to communism is yet another gift we receive at the hands of the poorest of the poor. Many thoughtful people have come to believe that the only hope for the world's suffering masses lies in the generation of fresh economic and social systems. It is widely held that the systems the developed world knows best are incapable of the self-cleansing it would take to make them universally beneficial. For reasons which need no amplification here, the rise of communism, the most widespread of these new systems, has not been very good news for Christians. Although one loathes any argument when communism is preceded by the word godless, nevertheless dialectical materialism denies the presence of God in history, and at that point is antithetical to the Christian faith.

Jose Miranda, perhaps the best New Testament scholar among liberation theologians, accepts as salvific much of what Marxism has to offer the poor of the world. At the same time he senses that Marxism fails to meet the elemental tests of biblical faith.

> In Marxist communism, there can be no justification for care of the old, the mentally retarded, the born cripples. The god known as productivity has no place for them in the world. How sad that precisely when the human being is at stake the Marxist foundations are inadequate. . . . What (Marx) failed to see is that providing for each according to his need presupposes caring for people simply because they exist, which in turn presupposes an absolute imperative unknown in his system of thought.[8]

Earlier in this century, under the dramatic missionary zeal of social activists, chiefly John R. Mott, a sturdy crew of idealistic young men and women became committed to: "win the world for Christ in our generation." This writer grew up believing that, "Christ is the hope of the world." Most of us who have taken a good look at the dynamics of history, particularly at what mischief the church has wrought in the underdeveloped world, have been forced to ask ourselves whether we can any longer make that affirmation. To the wretched of the earth—a designation which sadly includes most people—it began to appear that if Christ were not the hope of the world, perhaps Marx was.

Liberation theology may provide a significant alternative to a communism which has no room for God. Even among hard line capitalists and conservative Christians that ought to come as hopeful news. Liberation theology, as evidenced in the life and work of the church of the poor, may hold out for us, as well as for them, an escape from the terrible violence and bloodshed which seem inevitable. A third, yet undefined, economic and political mode may be needed to rechannel the energies which now are propelling us toward a universally devastating confrontation between the rival economic and political theories of the two super powers; each poised to obliterate life on this planet. It would not be the first time salvation has come from unlikely places. "Can anything good come out of Nazareth?" (John 1:46).

Only a failure to see what God is doing among the poor will permit us to engage in the reductionism which assumes liberation theology is inextricably linked to communism. While many liberationists use a Marxist analysis as their method of interpretation—hermeneutic—they remain essentially committed to the Christian gospel from which they draw their strength and their motivation. Liberation theology is not Marxism, although it is certainly not capitalism. It may offer a new, more equitable economics which is neither. My assumption is that Christ, not Marx, is still the hope of the world, but a Christ often hidden by systems which bear his name but deny his Spirit and way of life.

Another gift the base communities offer is the evidence they present of fresh ways to organize church life and work beyond the congregation. It may be that denominationalism is about to fade from the map of history. It has served us well, but its time to depart may be at hand. In its place may come other ecclesial structures more suited to our day. Base communities have discovered new ways of relating to each other which bypass ecclesiastical institutions smothered by bureaucratic inertia.

A decade ago we began to witness the slow demise of traditional ecumenical efforts. The conciliar movement found itself in deep trouble. In most communities traditional councils of churches went out of business, or gave way to more comprehensive social service agencies. Mergers between existing denominations were frozen in place. Work seemed to be halted on the major bridges linking Rome, the Orthodox and Protestantism. Congregations experienced a decrease in interest and support for these large ecumenical undertakings, while free and easy interchange of members diluted mainline denominational loyalties.

There were fresh winds. In local communities, without benefit of denominational sanction, there began to arise new avenues for inter-religious work and witness. Our best clues to the organization and conduct of extra-congregational work may come from models discovered in the base communities of the Third World, not from reports of prestigious ecclesiastical commissions.

Nothing is quite so exciting as watching a new idea about to be born. The newest, freshest, most inspiring Christian ideas of our age come to us as gifts from the wretched of the earth, Christ's people, those who received him gladly at his advent and who in our age still receive him gladly.

The final gift liberation theology offers is a fresh understanding of evangelism—a central theme of this book. To that theme, we now turn.

Notes

1. Gutierrez, *We Drink from Our Own Wells*. p. 125.
2. Gustavo Gutierrez, *A Theology of Liberation*. Orbis, 1973. p. 83.
3. *Ibid.* p. 26.
4. McElveney, *Good News*. p. 11.
5. Lee Cormie, *Challenge*. p. 26.
6. Leonardo Boff, *Church: Charism and Power*. SCM Press. p. 2.
7. *Ibid.* p. 2ff.
8. Jose Miranda, *Being and the Messiah*. Orbis, 1977. p. 37-8.

3

The Recovery of Evangelism

Evangelism is at a crisis point. No one who pays attention to what is or isn't going on in mainline churches needs to be convinced that things are serious and getting more so. Every year the statistical data is increasingly ominous: attendance down, baptisms down, new memberships down, Sunday schools way down. The most optimistic thing heard is: "I think we have bottomed out."

A yet unpublished study by the British sociologist Robert Towler entitled "Conventional Religion and Common Religion in Leeds," reveals that among those who claimed to be members of the Church of England, only 17 percent had been to a single worship service—apart from weddings or funerals—in an entire year. Free churches fared little better—27 percent. Almost half of all Roman Catholics had not darkened the door for mass.

Because of the phenomenal *success* of certain evangelical bodies, the statistics are probably somewhat higher in the United States. Yet among mainline denominations I doubt if much room could be found for euphoria. Interchurch organizations, which are the products and agents of the established churches, are faring no better. The National Council of Churches is continually faced with the condition St. Paul confronted when he wrote his desperate second letter to the church at Corinth, "We were [are] afflicted at every turn—fighting without and fear within" (2 Corinthians 7:5).

THE RECOVERY OF EVANGELISM 41

These same mainline churches are being outmaneuvered and outfinanced by an epidemic of militant fundamentalisms which stalk the land. Virulent new strains of old religious diseases have attacked the immune system of the U.S. psyche. They have learned how to infiltrate the media; we have not. They have discovered the value of computerized mailings; we have not. They have made comfortable alliances with the principalities and powers, and are rewarded handsomely for their allegiance; we have not.

I spent the spring and summer of 1985 in the United Kingdom. My first Sunday I attended the Anglican parish nearest my flat. It is a mammoth, gracious, old building with marvelous stained glass and the feeling of holiness about it. When the congregation had gathered for the main service of the day there were present: five members of the clergy and their assistants, six choristers, two ushers and an organist. The congregation only outnumbered the functionaries by a half dozen or so. While I subsequently encountered Anglican and Free Church parishes where there was considerable vitality, they were exceptions to the rule. I knew things had fallen off a bit. I had been to Britian five years before, but I was not prepared for the precipitious descent.

The situation in Western Europe is even more bleak. A West German pastor told me that in a parish which numbered 12,000 communicants, fewer than 40 could be expected on a Sunday morning. What is happening in Europe may be only a precursor of what we may experience in the United States. A Methodist pastor in California said that all that white you see when you cross the Rockies is not snow, but church letters thrown from cars by those moving west. If the megatrends observable in California are only a decade ahead of the rest of the nation, traditional denominations are in serious trouble.

A few years back the remedy became self-evident—*evangelism*. "We must recover our evangelistic enthusiasm." The reason for the decline, we told ourselves, was the assumption we could conduct business as usual in an age increasingly committed to secularism. Not so! But what was to be done? Certain styles were clearly counterproductive. Those churches which took the reformation of society seriously, and were concerned with peace, justice, women's rights and poverty were already on a slippery slope.

Most of the older ideas didn't work, were worn out, were far too unsophisticated, required too much effort or weren't popular among religious liberals in the first place. When is the last time your congregation built a brush arbor and held an open air revival? Or when did you even conduct a five-day preaching meeting inside your very respectable building? Revivalism was something someone else did, but not "our kind of churches." The crusades of the well known evangelists never did capture the attention or interest of most of us. Billy Graham was too much of a Bible belter for our tastes.

A few years back many of us had been through a variety of visitation campaigns. I remember spending three months organizing a congregation to "win 123 people to Christ" on one Sunday. We planned the work, and worked the plan and the plan worked! We beat our goal by three, and found ourselves with more additions to the church that one day than we had in the three prior years combined. If few among this newly washed throng had been confronted with the gospel, understood what membership in the body of Christ meant or were prepared to accept the responsibilities of the Christian faith, nevertheless they swelled attendance for a while. Sometime later, when the stick was pulled out of the water, we found it had left no hole. Now, in the 80s, visitation campaigns have gone out of style.

We might have tried the media and mass mailings. These blessings of the electronic age seemed to have served Moral Majority types well. That fact alone made us respectfully suspicious. Besides, we weren't nearly good enough stewards to afford such high-priced blitzes. Even if we had, our message seemed pale beside the show-biz styles of the biggies in the business.

"Something has to be done!" we kept repeating, as if the perpetuation of a lament would provide the answer. Since our revenues were not yet down as much as our attendance, and those of us who made our living from church were still receiving our salaries—increased salaries in many cases—we did little more than tell each other how bad things were.

Finally a group of astute souls, who were more like *us* than *them*, meaning the fundamentalists, hit upon a new answer. It was tagged church growth. It was simply the application to congregations of well tested marketing techniques. I doubt if anyone reading this book couldn't spell out the principles in a half dozen easy sentences.

1. Define your present constituency.
2. Locate those in the community who are already most like those you now have; that is, qualify your prospects.
3. Convince the congregation that among kinship and friendship networks there are many more non-churched people than they had realized.
4. Use the kinship and friendship networks to sell the product.
5. Generate new programs, groups and services within the life of the congregation, so that those who come in not only have their needs met, but discover ready-made niches where they can assume responsibility for and ownership of the program.
6. Don't divert your attention by allowing the congregation to do anything that will cast it in a negative light.

I believe every congregation ought to have a concentrated church growth program. If the problem is a diminution in attendance and participation, church growth techniques will reverse that trend. The church I serve is in a difficult downtown location in a static city. We have a church growth program much like the one outlined above; at least through step five, and we are growing. The growth may not be dramatic, but it is steady. Without church growth skills we would be shrinking.

Church growth provides a marvelous set of productive membership recruitment disciplines, *but it is not evangelism*. It has, in fact, become the trivialization of evangelism. Going out and finding people as much like we are as possible, and convincing them they are indeed our kind of folk, may be a wise sales strategy, but it is not the proclamation of the evangel. It is not the declaration of the liberating, freeing, saving, good news of Jesus Christ, to the end that persons and the societies in which persons live might be made whole, redeemed and used in service of the coming reign of God.

Church growth may allow for evangelism, or it may inhibit evangelism. Building up the institutional church may have a relationship to living in God's kingdom, or it may not. Left to its own devices the latter is probably more true. If evangelism has to do with radical transformation, church growth can well be counterproductive. If we are called to be unlike the once born of the world, simply bringing more of them in will not tend to recreate in Christ's image either them or us.

Not all growth is healthy. Some growths are malignancies; normal cells gone wild. A congregation known in the community as a bit odd, because it takes seriously things about which the principalities and powers are openly hostile, may not grow at all. If setting aside an active concern for the rights of women, homosexuals, the oppressed in Latin America, the black majority in South Africa and the poor in our own midst is done in the name of church growth, then church growth is anti-gospel and anti-evangelistic. If priorities for peace and disarmament, and the rights of the oppressed are played sotto voce for the sake of not rocking the boat into which we are crowding more and more of the half washed, then church growth is, in fact, demonic.

The problem we face is not the lack of evangelistic techniques, but the loss of the evangel! Ours is not an organizational problem, it is a theological problem. It is not that we have failed to identify and use the proper recruitment skills, but that we have lost the meaning of evangelism. But God has not left us without a witness. God has provided the poor to be our teachers. It is through the wretched of the earth we have an opportunity to recover both the evangel and the meaning of evangelism.

Evangelism is the fruit of Christian praxis. It has little to do with getting people to join our churches. That is only one possible result of evangelism, and not the most important one at that. It is God who adds to the church those who are being saved (Acts 2:47). When we are faithful to the gospel, God gives the increase. In a society openly hostile to the radical message of the gospel, we should not expect a church which proclaims it to win popularity contests. Every congregation must ask itself whether it is ready to take that risk, which is itself a liberating act of faith.

"I will build my church," Matthew 16:18. God has acted in Jesus Christ and continues to act through the Holy Spirit to redeem persons and societies of persons. Evangelism is God's work. We share in that gracious work as we proclaim in word and act the appearance and reality of the Messianic age. We point to outbreakings of the kingdom, not only in our particular location, but wherever they are evidenced. In our era that means among the poor.

The evangel calls persons, and the societies in which persons live, to wholeness, to the power, joy and freedom of the gospel. It invites whosoever will to share in God's redemptive work, and enter God's gracious reign. It declares the good news that God has already offered freedom from our sins and their consequences. It calls men and women to become new creatures, born again citizens of a new order. It is to our shame that we let the term, "born again" be taken over by those who have utterly abused it. It rightly belongs in the vocabulary of liberation theology, which invites new creatures to share in a new creation.

While evangelism is an individual matter, it is also a corporate matter. It is more than winning them one by one. Christ came to save, redeem and set free the world. A slave is not set free until something happens to his chains and to the system which enslaved him in the first place. While not downplaying the importance of personal conversion, liberation theology demonstrates that both in the Bible and throughout Christian history God called entire societies to wholeness. It was the nation which was time and again called to repentance and faithfulness.

As Croatto says:

> God's salvific activity is collective; it starts on the political and social level and ends on that level. The liberation of the Israelites in Egypt was an event with political and social consequences. God did not begin by saving in the spiritual sphere, not even from sin. He saves the total man, whose human realization he himself, or other men who abuse their power and social status, may hinder.[1]

Evangelism does not produce the kingdom. It rather points to evidences of God's kingdom. It works through earthbound projects, which are only a foretaste of the kingdom. The project entrusted to us is to establish a social order in which healing replaces brokenness in the affairs of men and women; liberation overcomes oppression; justice prevails over injustice; life breaks out in places where death has ruled.

As Hugo Echegaray puts it:
> The kingdom comes not to explain the world, but to transform it; it comes to human beings in order to reveal the Father to them, that is, to reveal the God who makes them the object and aim of his love and who is therefore a power that does away with all the conditions preventing full human growth.[2]

Jesus' declaration at the synagogue in Nazareth was evangelistic. When John the Baptist announced that the kingdom of God was at hand, and Jesus later described its signs, the evangel had come to birth. Here was an open invitation to live as born again men and women in the new Messianic age.

The church has always held this treasure in its earthen vessels. The breaking forth of the kingdom into human affairs is what we pray for every time we gather, in whatever language, under whatever secular flag or in whatever economic system. The Lord gave the disciples revolutionary words when they asked him how to pray. It is that prayer which pleads to God that the new reality Jesus talked about in the parables and in the Sermon on the Mount might come on earth, as it is in heaven. Christians who are afraid of revolution, afraid of what might happen if the system which allows some to be overfed and most to be hungry is replaced by a system in which equity is the norm, ought to cease offering the Lord's prayer. They would be better off settling for "Now I lay me down to sleep. . . ." For to utter the Lord's Prayer, but to resist the petition which is at its heart, is blasphemy.

We must repeat; a redeemed society is only a foretaste of the kingdom. The kingdom is far beyond any social order we can either design or implement. The kingdom is an eschatological reality. It is God prevailing over sin, pain and death. In its plenitude it brings the time when, "the earth will be [is] filled with the knowledge of the glory of the LORD as the waters cover the sea" (Habakkuk 2:14). We may pray for its coming, live as if it were a reality, reshape our common life to conform to its demands, but it is God's to establish.

Leonardo Boff warned against the temptation to see as identical salvation and social reform:
> Liberation in Jesus Christ is not identified *with* political, economic and social liberation, but it is historically identified *in* political, economic and social liberation.³

This liberation of the whole person and the whole order of reality moves beyond the temporal. In the 1975 encyclical, *Evangelli Nuntiandi*, released in the midst of the first struggles between the Vatican and the Latin American theologians, Paul VI insisted that salvation must include social justice. Although in some encounters with Third World theologians the Pope seemed to warn the faithful that the overpolitization of the church was to be avoided, the preponderance of his texts affirmed the fundamental work the theologians were doing. The Pope included both politics and the final redemption of history when he wrote that the core of evangelization is "salvation in Jesus Christ . . . that has its beginning in this life and will come to total completion in eternity" (Section 27).

Our project may be a temporal and political one, but the kingdom toward which the project points is an eschatological and eternal one. "Whatever you bind [is bound] on earth shall be [is] bound in heaven, and whatever you loose [is loosed] on earth shall be [is] loosed in heaven" (Matthew 16:19). Evangelism leads to salvation, and salvation is more than a reordering of society. That is why salvation can never be reduced to social reconstruction. But neither can there be legitimate evangelism that does not call for men and women to turn from sinful societal structures, and embrace Messianic social ethics. In the words of Leonardo Boff:
> The larger horizon is salvation. It's against that horizon that liberation is situated. Liberation doesn't embrace, cover, include salvation. Salvation includes liberation, penetrates it and spills out beyond it on all sides. The broader reality . . . of liberation is salvation . . . Liberation is the political dimension of salvation.⁴

Gutierrez has it:
> Although the Kindgom must not be confused with the

establishment of a just society, this does not mean that it is indifferent to this society. Nor does it mean that this just society constitutes a "necessary condition" for the arrival of the kingdom, nor that they are closely linked, nor that they converge. More profoundly, the announcement of the kingdom reveals to society itself the aspiration for a just society and leads it to discover unsuspected dimensions and unexplored paths. The Kingdom is realized in a society of brotherhood and justice; and, in turn, this realization opens up the promise and hope of complete communion of all men with God. The political is grafted into the eternal.[5]

One only needs to reflect on how Jesus described the signs of the kingdom of which he was the herald. He said it would be evidenced as the poor are blessed, the meek inherit the earth and the peacemakers called God's children. In God's reign the last go first and the first last; there are no insiders nor are there outcasts; no servant and no master. All the normal ways of doing things are stood on their heads. In the kingdom good is returned for evil, enemies redeemed by love; the Samaritans, non persons, are welcomed as saints; the chief among us becomes the servant of all and Lazarus, whose sores the dogs licked as he begged by the gate, rests in Abraham's bosom. In God's kingdom it is the wayward son who is welcomed home, given the robe, the ring, the fatted calf and the party. In the kingdom no one hurts or destroys in all God's holy mountain.

While we in the privileged world struggle with honing the proper marketing techniques, and call that trivilization evangelism, God is at work with the wretched of the earth, the poor and the oppressed actualizing the Messianic age. It is from them we learn what evangelism is about.

Liberationists teach us that to proclaim the Lordship of Christ is far more than getting people to accept a doctrine about him. The task of evangelism is not to inform the world, but to call it to repentance and redemption. The evangelistic message is not found in right words, or right beliefs,—orthodoxy, but in saving acts—orthopraxis. Jesus did not come into the world to give it a new set of doctrines, but to set it free. He brought salvation by what he did in his life, and by laying down his life.

To the extent the individual confession that Jesus is the Messiah also involves engaging with him in his salvific work, personal conversion and building up the church may lead to evangelism. As Jose Miranda puts it:

> To believe that this man, Jesus of Nazareth, is the Messiah is to believe that in him the messianic kingdom has arrived. It is to believe that in our age the kingdom of God has arrived, an event which fulfills all hopes[6].

Thus salvation is a liberating encounter with God, an encounter demonstrated both by the rebirthing of persons and the reshaping of society.

"Radical liberation is the gift which Christ offers us. By his death and resurrection he redeems man from sin and all its consequences."[7] This terse summary by Gutierrez defines our evangelistic message. It requires no great theological mind to see how far removed this notion of evangelism is from church growth. The former has to do with the whole gospel. The latter is the announcement that "you have found a church of friendly people, who share your goals, are very much like you are now and stand ready to meet your needs."

Insofar as we confront individuals with the meaning of church membership, but do not confront them with the claims of Christ and the wider dimensions of the gospel, we have deceived them. It may be that instead of enlisting them in the church, we have only identified for their use a convenient neighborhood club.

The question persists: How do we transform our congregations from groups of friendly folks, who welcome, indeed go out and seek like-spirited and congenial potential members to come swell the ranks, into instruments of evangelism? As William McElveney puts it:

> How can a membership campaign that features positive thinking for the privileged and prosperous regenerate into an outreaching love for the social and

economic lepers of the world? Evangelism is escapist if it has nothing to say to the affluence of the privileged and prosperous amid Third World starvation. Evangelism is expedient when it traffics in easy formulas and safe doctrines instead of calling us to a discipleship of transformed values. If evangelism conceals the cost of discipleship when it should reveal the call to obedience, are we going to rejoice in a quantitative kingdom of business as usual?[8]

Perhaps the initial task in the reshaping of congregational life is a simple organizational one. Perhaps we first realign the structure so that legitimate efforts to increase the size of the congregation are not confused with efforts to act out the good news of Jesus Christ. The first is important. Without the second, however, whatever goes on is not church. We might begin by establishing a Commission on Evangelism which has nothing to do with church growth. The unit seeking to enlarge the membership can then be called what it is, a "Commission on Membership Recruitment." At least the lines of demarcation will be clear.

Evangelism is then free to annouce the liberating, saving good news of Jesus Christ wherever men and women are in captivity, be they in the slums of Mexico City or the board rooms of U.S. corporations. Evangelism is thus loosed from the pit of marketing devices and membership recruitment drives into which it has lamentably fallen.

An hour's drive from Beijing stands the magnificent residence of the Dowager Empress, who presided over the final days of imperial China. It is called, "The Summer Palace," and was the site of enormous garden parties for the elite of the Chi'ng dynasty. Now it belongs to the people, who visit it by the millions, all looking around proudly as if to say: "This is mine now." In the center of the estate is a lake, and in the lake stands the imperial Chinese navy. The Dowager was told that unless she rebuilt the fleet, China would not be safe from her traditional enemies. When Japanese gunboats subsequently arrived there was no naval defense. The Dowager had commissioned, however, this one ship. It was made of concrete, and was really a pier jutting out from the cluster of elegant buildings on the shoreline. Its purpose was to host extravaganzas for the nobles of the land. To it they flocked in as great a number as had been invited.

The church is Christ's navy, commissioned both to search the sea for the shipwrecked, and to make the ocean a safer place for those who sail on it. Massive, immobile concrete ships, sitting in the tranquility of inland lakes and built for the enjoyment of "our kind of people" may add a bit of charm to the scenery, but they will have little affect on the drowning.

Notes

1. Andrew J. Kirk, *Liberation Theology: An Evangelical View from the Third World.* John Knox Press, 1979. pp. 38-9.
2. Hugo Echegaray, *The Practice of Jesus.* Orbis, 1984. p. 88.
3. Leonardo and Clodovis Boff, *Salvation and Liberation.* Orbis, 1984. p. 33.
4. *Ibid.* pp. 102-3.
5. Gutierrez, *A Theology.* pp. 231-2.
6. Jose Miranda, *Marx and the Bible.* Orbis, 1974. p. 208.
7. Gutierrez, *A Theology.* p. 176.
8. McElveney, *Good News.* p. 88.

4
The Liberation of Persons

Although liberation theology is focused on social or structural renewal, theology cannot avoid the question of individuals and their captivities. If liberation theology is to address those in the developed world, the world of the middle class, it must have something to say about persons as well as about institutions and social structures.

Not that the contemporary North American church has lost sight of persons. In much of our church life that is all one hears. Two sorts of rampant religious individualism abound. One kind is an other worldly: "Get me to heaven, dear Jesus" or "Please be my personal friend, Lord, because I love you so much."

The impact of this cuddling with Jesus' religiosity comes crashing through on what is known as "Christian radio." Torch songs to Jesus have even invaded public worship, under the guise of contemporary Christian music. "It's you and me Jesus"—the English is even terrible—"all the way from here to glory." On both sides of the Atlantic, congregations are divided over the inclusion of pop songs in worship. Hymnbooks vie with one another for space in pew racks, and which one is used depends on who is planning a particular service. Some of the lyrics are quite acceptable, and we should always be ready to adopt tunes from the popular idiom. After all, Bach did and so did Luther. But lyrics which describe a relationship with Jesus in almost erotic terms evidence Western individualism gone wild.

The church has often suffered from theologically repulsive hymns, even though musicians with some sense of the faith continually try to clean up the hymnals. The current vacuous sentimentalism seems to be a reaction to the dullness and lack of spiritual power in the traditional churches. The diagnosis may be accurate, but the prescription is unpalatable.

The other sort of galloping individualism tends to be smoother—more the peddling of the psychology of success than of Christian teaching. Consider the following sermon titles: "Ten Keys to the Happy Life," "How to Overcome Shyness" and "Turning Your Troubles into Sunbeams." The profundity of the human dilemma, the despair of the poor and even the cross are never mentioned, lest they get in the way of affirmative feelings about both self and the preacher serving up the psychological niceties.

Our preoccupation with individualism is one reason why it has been so difficult for the average parishioner to hear the gospel of liberation. As Richard Schaull says:

> It would hardly occur to us that we should seek God in and through our relationship with other persons, much less in and through our relationship with the poor, broken and marginalized. . . . In evangelical Protestantism we speak of finding God in a highly charged emotional experience; in both Catholic and Protestant circles our language about God is grounded in Greek conceptualizations. God exists in us as we develop the right concepts.[1]

Nevertheless, one cannot lose sight of the person and stay in sight of the gospel. Obviously Jesus, in his liberating ministry, was profoundly concerned with individuals. We have their names, or at least descriptions which detail their uniqueness: Mary Magdalene, a rich young ruler, Lazarus, Martha, Zacchaeus, a centurian. With the exception of the ten lepers, persons were healed one at a time: a man born blind, a woman with a flow of blood, a man with a withered arm, a demoniac who lived in the caves.

Jesus' healing miracles were not simply good deeds offered to the needy; they were good works, evidences of the Messianic age.

If one of the major themes of liberation thought is the identification and celebration of these outcroppings, then miracles which offer evidence of God's kingdom cannot be ignored, whether they are addressed to social units or to individuals. Jose Miranda puts it this way:

> They [Jesus' miracles] were messianic "good works." They implied the terrifyingly revolutionary thesis that this world of contempt and oppression can be changed into a world of complete selflessness and unrestricted mutual assistance . . . The "good works" of the Messiah did not consist in giving what was left over, in distributing the surplus of a civilization that in itself remains untouched by the distribution. . . . Society acclaims and venerates charitable works. . . . The "good works" described in the gospels have to be the object of "the world's" hatred; otherwise there is no gospel, . . . no good news. Like the Messiah they are welcome only to "those who have been born of God," that is, to those who are dedicated to the love of neighbor and the achievement of justice.[2]

If Miranda goes further than we might like in his insistence that the healing miracles were revolutionary, not compassionate acts, nevertheless he also makes clear they were more than the noblesse oblige of heaven's richest peer. Laying aside our need to intellectualize, it seems obvious that the gospel writers were telling us that Jesus had compassion on the suffering, not that he claimed to be the Son of God. The theological implications were added later.

Jesus' care for and his healing of individuals demonstrated God's action on behalf of oppressed persons; in many cases persons who were physically bound. The good news of the gospel for the blind and the lame, as well as for the poor, was embodied—acted out—good news. The gospel was not good advice, but God's good works. As Miranda reminds us:

> The good news called the gospel is not Greek news. It is the most purely biblical news that can be imagined. It is a word signifying action, not information; it seeks to *achieve what it says*, not simply to notify.[3]

Part of our incapacity to hear the gospel as action, and not as doctrine, is that we are still Greeks. When people in our congregations want to know the truth, they mean a fact, a bit of provable data they can accept intellectually; wisdom, if it is public; gnosis, if it is mysterious. But the good news of the kingdom is not good advice, a new idea or the unveiling of wisdom, but works of love and power. "Go and tell John what you hear and see: the blind receive their sight and the lame walk, lepers are cleansed and the deaf hear, and the dead are raised up, and the poor have good news preached to them" (Matthew 11:4-5).

In the pivotal story of the Exodus, the presence of God is known in acts which freed a people in bondage; in the ministry of Jesus it is known in acts which freed individuals from their chains, diseases and even from the grave. Christian praxis, doing the truth not just describing it, demonstrates the outbreaking of the kingdom on behalf of the oppressed collectively or individually. God acts for us. The word becomes flesh in our midst. God forgives all our iniquities and heals all our diseases. The good news is not something God addresses to us in word, but something God gives in deed, by the working of the Spirit. The activism suggested not only in the book of James, but throughout the epistles, calls Christians to reflect the incarnation in their lives. We are to act the way God acts, "not love in word and speech, but in deed and truth" (1 John 3:18).

Against this background, one looks at the contemporary church. I speak, as I have throughout this book, to the middle-class, mainline congregations in the developed world, to the typical gathering in Middletown, U.S. or Bampton, England. If we are to be faithful to the liberating gospel of Christ, every congregation needs to be involved in healing ministries. Not as the hyped up "look what I can do," of the media oriented faith healers, but as that which evidences the victory, the liberating power of God over every human enemy.

I believe the ministry of healing parallels the ministry of social reform; consider the book of "The Acts of the Apostles." It might have been called "Evidences of the Kingdom of God," for that is its theme. The author of this second part of the narrative of Jesus' life and the ongoing work of the community of faith, picks up the story by declaring that the content of Jesus' teaching after the resurrection was the same as it had been prior to the events of the passion. "To them he presented himself alive after his passion by many proofs, appearing to them during forty days, and speaking of the kingdom of God" (Acts 1:3).

If the apostles were faithful to what their master had taught them, and the church assumes they were, it is certain the apostolic community believed that the manifestations of the kingdom of which the Lord had spoken would be evidenced in their midst. There would be signs and wonders, even greater than the mighty works he had done. The miracles of the book of Acts were an extension of the works of Jesus—evidences, outcroppings of God's sovereignty. An agent had been provided. It was the breath or Spirit of God.

The chronicler details the events of Pentecost, the day on which the Messianic age began to achieve the visible identity which shortly thereafter came to be known as the church. He then quickly moves to a description of evidences beginning in chapter 3. Peter and John, devout Jews as was their teacher, had gone to the temple to pray. En route they were accosted by a man who had been lame since birth. He had been carried to a particular temple gate by his friends in order to beg. Even today the areas surrounding significant places of worship are choice locations for that kind of endeavor. Assuming the apostles were only a pair of pious Jews, he called out for alms. What he got was quite different. Peter "directed his gaze at him" (v. 4). It is safe to assume that after what had occurred on Pentecost, Peter's gaze was far more than a curious stare. Such a look encouraged the man to believe that a generous gift was not far behind. He was correct in his assumption, but wrong as to the nature of the gift.

"I have no silver and gold, but I give you what I have; in the name of Jesus of Nazareth, walk!" (v. 6). The man was restored, and Peter took the occasion to proclaim that in Jesus, who had been crucified, something new in history had made an appearance. It was new, yet it was related to Jewish history. Here was a visible sign that the Messianic age was now operative. The evidence was observable to anyone near the temple gate that afternoon (Acts 3:1-16).

Note, this was not a faith healing. As is the case in many of the healing stories in the gospels, there is no indication the man healed had faith in Jesus, or had even heard of him. The only faith alluded to is the faith of the apostles. The healing takes place, not because the lame man had gotten doctrinal wisdom or came to trust in the name of Jesus, but because the kingdom of God was being displayed through mighty signs and wonders. The succeeding verses attest that this was but the first of many signs and wonders.

Granted all the critical hurdles one must jump to bring that story to life in the modern church, a comparison with how we now do things is of considerable interest. In the simple sentence uttered by Peter there are two remarkable divergences from the acts of the modern church. In the first place we can no longer honestly say, "We have no silver and gold." The truth is, we've plenty of it. Your congregation has plenty of it, despite protestations you might make to the contrary. We know how to treat the suffering people of our communities and the world. We take up a collection. We spend hundreds of millions of dollars a year for the alleviation of human misery, and so we should. Nothing in the story suggests that it would have been inappropriate to have given the man material relief. The fact is, the apostles had none to give. Jesus often talked about providing financial assistance to the poor. During his ministry a money box had been kept for that purpose.

It is the second disparity which highlights the first. We can no longer say, "In the name of Jesus of Nazareth, walk!" Since we now can provide silver and gold, we believe we have appropriately responded to human need. But at the same time it means we no longer even consider offering the more important gift, the gift of healing. If the gospel offers liberation from those captivities which oppress individuals, we need to recapture the larger gift.

This is not to suggest we take up faith healing. Healing, either in the larger social context, or for individuals, may not be a product of the faith of society or the individual at all. It may rather be an evidence of God's continuing activity in human history. What usually passes for faith healing may be sorcery at worst and psychological manipulation at best. Although in Acts and in the gospels we find accounts where faith and healing are related, what I am suggesting is not of that sort. The church has been given the gift of healing because the kingdom is in our midst, not because exquisite devotion is evidenced by the one healed, or even by the church in whose midst the healing takes place. Liberation comes as God's gift. We celebrate that gift by our active response. Both social reformation and individual healings are among the results.

As much as we may complain about the Oral Robertses of the world, we have produced them by having abdicated healing ministries. We have failed to evidence the reality of the kingdom, and have turned healing over to scientists, on one hand, and faith healers on the other. One might argue that there is room for both, although my natural prejudices generate some suspicion of the latter. But if liberation theology identifies the mighty acts of God as evidences of the kingdom, as does the New Testament, then what is true for the politically oppressed as a group may be just as true for the bodily oppressed as individuals.

As do an increasing number of congregations, the one I serve has a healing ministry. It is not advertised widely, nor is it emotionally manipulative. It does not call on people to bundle up their faith in a tight little ball, shut their eyes and believe God will make them well. People do get well, in a number of ways: physically, emotionally, relationally, spiritually, vocationally and more. But it is not because they get or already have more faith than others. The healings that take place are evidences of the Messianic age. Nor do we confuse healings with cures. Many people are healed and not cured. Sometimes the healing comes, after a long struggle, in the form of death.

Ours is a quiet prayer service. It is similar to services in parishes and ecumenical gatherings throughout the world. Most of the prayers are read. There are extended periods of free prayer when we pray for others by name. We always include in our prayers those in difficult places and situations. We cannot have a service without praying for the oppressed far beyond the confines of our church.

In an earlier chapter we described how the base communities of the poor were formed in Latin America. We offered a quasi-fictional example. Do you remember the initial focus of that group in Nueva? Bible study! And what did they discover? Evidences of God at work in history, standing by the oppressed and delivering them from their oppression. Our service focuses on that kind of Bible study with the identical discovery. God stands with the beaten, the wounded, the diseased, the afflicted, the wretched of the earth. And when we realize we are indeed beaten, wounded, diseased, afflicted and wretched, we discover that God stands by us.

The core group or basic community is called "The Ebb Tide Fellowship." It is a collection of those whose lives—physically, emotionally, relationally—are at some low point and those who are in solidarity with them in their distress. After the Bible study, and after we have prayed for others, the opportunity is given for those present to kneel in the midst of the assembly and receive the laying on of hands, as we ask for healing. And healing takes place. I have knelt in the midst of the group, and have experienced the kingdom's outbreaking in my life. One time I was recovering from a physical illness. A second time was the week after the accidental death of my son. I was a broken man. I knelt, the hands of God's people were laid on me, and I began to be restored.

The Ebb Tide Fellowship is not a group of economically deprived people, although God has provided a few very poor persons, who often act as our mentors. If we chose to do so, we could take up a sizable collection for the alleviation of human misery. In fact, the members of the group tend to be dedicated stewards. But of more importance, they are also able to say "in the name of Jesus of Nazareth, walk!"

Where did we discover we had that gift? Not from the spiritualists, or faith healers or mystics, although each added a dimension, but from the wretched of the earth.

Middle-class people suffer many other forms of oppression. If the gospel is given to all so that all might be set free, then the gift of liberation is given to the church to use for the glory of God and the freedom of persons in whatever circumstance or under whatever social conditions they live. The concluding sections of this chapter will describe three well-known captivities which bind middle-class individuals.

The first of the trilogy is boredom—the general sense of nondirection and meaninglessness which afflicts modern life. I do not consider psychotherapy to be one of my mature gifts. Yet more of my time is consumed in counseling than any other single function, with the possible exception of study and writing. The problems faced by many of those I encounter can be summed up in the phrase "spiritual ennui." Nothing in life means very much. They are bored with their jobs, and on the perpetual lookout for either another or ways to spend less and less time and energy on the one they have. They are bored with their families and look for meaning in extramarital relationships which often prove to be as enervating as what they have sought to escape. Yet many who find themselves involved in these affairs, don't know how to get out of what they don't know how they got into.

Persons stricken with spiritual ennui find it difficult to have a good time at anything. Perhaps to a greater degree than any mass culture in history, affluent U.S. middle-class folk have more spare time and more money to us, as they please, but little they can do, no place they can go and nothing they can buy seems to fill the gray void.

How are their days shaped? Arising with a slight headache; looking at the non-news while eating a non-breakfast; traveling much too far to a job which provides little fulfillment; doing it, or at least getting through the day; traveling much too far to get back home; sitting down before the television with a beer, or two, or six while "the wife" fixes dinner; eating as silently as Orthodox monks, while watching reruns of *Gilligan's Island*; moving slowly to the couch in the same "family room" before the same household deity until they fall asleep; lumbering into a sexless bedroom and getting up in the morning to go through the same routine. Weekends are spent similarly, only without the need to make the two long daily trips and suffer the boredom which takes place between them.

What I have described is the male manifestation of ennui. Increasing numbers of women suffer a similar disease of the spirit, with a slightly different set of symptoms. Although I can cite no clinically reliable data to support the contention, it is my impression that many women have managed to escape, at least in degree if not in kind, the most destructive aspects of the captivity. Permit me a passing observation; not a revealed matter of faith. Among those who have discovered "women's liberation" there has come at least a modicum of relief from the oppressive grayness which afflicts so many middle-class men.

I must admit there have been occasional long evenings when I have had a taste of ennui. The family is out. It has been a long day. I have used my mind to the maximum. I have nothing in my basement shop which cries out for attention. I pour a drink and turn on the television. In my bourgeois world I have been provided with a gadget which allows me to change channels without leaving my chair. Before I am aware of it, I find myself mindlessly pushing the button over and over watching ten channels at once and watching nothing. Slowly I become conscious that I am exquisitely bored. I can only imagine how it must be to live like that every evening, day after day, week after week.

If these people are not oppressed in the way it takes form among the poor, neither are they free. They are, in fact, possessed by all the things they own. They cannot shake the structures of their bondage. They are simultaneously the slaves and the Egyptians.

The captivity which devolves from the luxuries of middle-class life is not to be compared with the oppression faced by those tens of millions of people without the basic necessities. It is with considerable misgiving I have included in a book about liberation theology these modest captivities of the affluent, and I ask pardon from those who deal with and live in the midst of grinding poverty. But if to exist as if life had no meaning is to be in chains, the oppressions of the middle class are only different in intensity from the oppressions of the poor. Or, as we suggested earlier, if it is not oppression from which we suffer, it is at least to be unfree.

In working with those who are enslaved by spiritual ennui, liberation theology has significantly changed the way I do pastoral counseling. Obviously occasions arise when the best psychological skills and tools available are appropriate and usable. But in situations such as the one described, these tools are useless. I doubt if five years of psychoanalysis would provide the answer to many of those trapped by spiritual ennui. The remedy is rather theological. These people need to be set free from their bondage to sin and death, and offered the joys of God's kingdom. Their healing does not come through clinical insights I can provide into the nature of their problems. My task is not to approach their captivities from a psycho dynamic perspective, but to tell them about the gospel; to introduce them to the one who can set them free.

This is a way we are called to do personal evangelism. I am fully aware of the dangers involved in using the counseling session as a site for evangelism, but I am persuaded that the opportunity to help people be set free by the Spirit is far more important than the possibility we will abuse the trust of those who come to us with personal problems. I usually find this approach appropriate only after many hours of careful and creative listening, which means I have not totally abandoned usual pastoral counseling tools even in these situations.

Obviously there are a limited number of counselees for whom direct personal evangelism is appropriate, although it is my assumption that the number is much larger than most of us might admit. For many a breakthrough often comes when they hear and believe the good news of the liberating power of God. Often my task is to direct them to a base community; in our case, the Ebb Tide Fellowship. As they pray, learn to study the Bible, feel surrounded and touched by others, many of whom face or have faced the same debilitating grimness, liberation takes place. Freedom comes, not because either they or the community suddenly discover in themselves a quality of faith not known before, but because they experience the work of God, the outbreaking of the kingdom in their midst.

The second example of how liberation theology speaks to individual captivities concerns those ensnarled by alcohol and drug abuse. All my previous pastoral experience with alcoholics had been an exercise in futility. I doubt if I had been successful in helping a single one dry out, at least for long. In recent years, however, I have become more aware of the good work done by Alcoholics Anonymous (AA). Without entering into a debate about the merits or demerits of the way AA goes at things, I have discovered it to be far more effective in dealing with problem drinkers, and their families, than I had ever been. Our congregation houses a large AA chapter, which meets throughout the week. I tend to view these units as basic communities, with highly specific projects. The analogy may be limited, but in some sense we have here the church of the poor. Here persons discover in study, in a recognition of their own hopelessness, in an appeal to their "higher power" and in their relationship to one another, a way out of their captivity. In the safety of a caring community they are allowed to turn loose of that which has bound them. It may seem like a trivial matter to those who have never been afflicted with alcoholism, or intimately involved with someone who has, but in our culture there are few more widespread, grave and dehumanizing captivities.

Our congregation is known as a place where people who face all kinds of destructive life forces are welcomed. We do not stand in judgment on alcoholics. We welcome them as brothers and sisters seeking freedom from their chains, just as all of us seek freedom from one set of chains or another. As alcoholics are made whole, and move beyond the privatized phase of their healing, the congregation is able to celebrate their sobriety. Several members of the congregation have left our community to work in agencies dealing with substance abuse. Everyone of them has been a former alcoholic or drug addict. Ours, you must remember, is a very proper middle class church. When they depart, just as we do with others who leave the city, they are invited to the front of the congregation where we tell the story of their liberation and commission them as emissaries of the gospel. Theirs is the story of another outbreaking of the Messianic age; another incident in which the church has been able to say, by the power of the Holy Spirit, "even if we have silver and gold, giving it to you wouldn't set you free. We have something far better to offer. In the name of Jesus of Nazareth, walk!"

The third captivity which binds the middle class of the First World may be more closely related to our affluence than are ennui or alcoholism. It is what I shall call, the prophylactic life. It is a life without risk, without adventure. It is the well protected, safe, orderly, careful life. Boundaries are tightly set. What one does today will look very much like what one did in a lifetime of yesterdays. Little recognition exists that there can be greater joy, deeper spirituality or the radical reformation of anything.

I read Hal Luccock's sermon, "Marching off the Map," almost four decades ago, but its impact has stuck with me. Luccock described how the Roman armies just kept going when they came to the end of the map and were faced with a great blank area labeled "unknown." The text was Hebrews 11:8, "By faith Abraham obeyed when he was called to go out to a place which he was to receive as an inheritance; and he went out, not knowing where he was to go." Not much of that is seen these days, at least not by the very careful people who occupy the pews in most of our mainline churches.

The prophylactic life probably came into the Judeo-Christian tradition when the people of God traded in the tabernacle for the temple. The tabernacle was portable. It could travel anywhere the Lord wanted the people to go. It could be taken down in a day or two and moved over the next valley or hill.

The temple, on the other hand, was immovable, sturdy, nailed down, conservative. It never budged. Institutions set in concrete, either figuratively or actually, at their inception or shortly thereafter become rigid and inflexible. The modern parish tends to be more like a temple than a tabernacle. Think how much of your church budget is spent in the care and feeding of your building. Enormous amounts of money, which might otherwise be used to alleviate the misery of the world, are consumed in maintaining structures which are immobile. Our institutions, as well as the steel and concrete which house them, devour our capacity to march off the map, or even venture very close to its border.

The greater problem is this: once we build large institutions—speaking of the size of our memberships and complexity of our programs—we tend to limit by direct ratio the risks these institutions are willing to take. One of the inarticulated rules of church growth is "Don't rock the boat." Radicial action and church growth often seem antithetical. Every parish needs to decide whether it is to be a temple or a tabernacle. The larger it is, the more it will tend to be temple and the more it will rely on its substantial contributors just to keep the roof repaired and the furnace in operation.

It doesn't take a large church, however, to be more temple than tabernacle. Some of the most rigid, constricted, mummified congregations I know are very small, ruled by one or two people whose vision of the kingdom died long ago. They lead prophylactic lives and make certain the congregations they control do so as well.

Even so, the willingness to march off maps is probably higher in the smaller units. The base communities described in chapter two are never larger than can be gotten into a humble home, just a few families at most. Their poverty sanctions a joyful acceptance of a revolutionary gospel they might not enjoy if they had accounts and buildings and institutional paraphernalia to maintain and protect. Their rejection of prophylactic living allows them to be among the most dynamic of all contemporary church institutions.

The parallel is easily drawn between institutions and individuals. It is difficult for most of us to take risks. We have too much to lose. If I have a large mortgage on my home, two car payments, and all the other accoutrements which go with middle-class life, there is not much room for risk taking. I will hold onto that boring life-draining job at all costs. I will stay within carefully prescribed boundaries. I will be owned, lock, stock and barrel, by my house, my cars and other gadgets of bourgeois life.

A colleague of mine was being paid a salary he believed too modest to stretch over the expectations of the middle-class congregation in which he worked, let alone his material ambitions. He was faced with three alternatives. He could find some way to increase his income. He could try to cut his expenses. He could march off the map. He took the third option. He sold everything he had, not to provide money for the poor, but to pay his creditors, and with his family went out not even knowing where he was to go.

In the years since, the members of that family have been full unpaid workers in the peace movement. They write and perform music, make speeches and spend time in jail as the result of acts of civil disobedience. As long as he had to worry about how he was going to pay his bill at the local golf course, not to mention the bank, he was trapped. He had to live a prophylactic life. He was liberated only when he decided not to be a middle-class consumer. He and his family live in a farmhouse in exchange for doing some chores for the woman who owns the place but no longer occupies the house. They heat by wood stove, and read by kerosene lantern. They haul water from an outside pump. Although they have found support in a local congregation, they have also developed a base community of two families which live as a single vocational unit.

One can see why it was tough for the rich young ruler to follow Jesus: "For he had great possessions" (Mark 10:22). Jesus did not infer that it was impossible for a rich man to enter the kingdom of heaven, only difficult. Just as with poor institutions, personal poverty is no guarantee that one will abandon the prophylactic life. As the small church can be immobile, so can the poverty stricken person. I have always believed the saddest man in all the stories Jesus told was the one-talent chap who hid his money in the ground because he was afraid (Matthew 15:25).

Nevertheless, the consumerism which dominates our culture may define one of our most compelling captivities. Dorothee Soelle suggests that for us:

> life is entirely expressed within the culture of consumerism.... I have often heard American tourists who traveled in countries behind the Iron Curtain say, "Look at those empty show windows.... Life isn't worthwhile here...." The prevailing consumerism [is] a new fascism because it simply destroys all human values softly, without physical violence.... Our need for liberation [from consumerism] has a different starting point than the struggle for economic justice. Our being exploited is different from the exploitation of the Third World. Still, it is one beast that rules over us ... we in the affluent societies tend to overlook its fascist dimensions. Our immediate experience of the beast is of its hedonistic side rather than of its oppressive side.[4]

The liberating Christ, who promised to set us free from every captivity, can also rescue us from the consumer oriented prophylactic life. Our project is to become a risk taking people, march off a few maps, radicalize our lives and our work, confront the principalities and powers and rulers of this present generation with the saving, freeing news of the gospel.

It will probably not happen in churches unless within them there are small groups willing to demonstrate the freedom which comes with risk taking. It is quite unlikely, for instance, that entire congregations will join in an aggressive witness for disarmament. But there must be room in every congregation for small units, base communities of people who will. In the congregation I serve we have what is known as the "Shalom Task Force." This group helped organize a petition drive calling on the city council to adopt a resolution concerning a nuclear freeze. The group was wise enough to realize that there were similar small groups in other parishes throughout the city. The political strength of the base community develops as networks are formed.

Ours is a very conservative place. Left to their own predilections, not a member of the city council would vote for such a resolution. When confronted with several thousand signatures and a chamber full of people, the vote was "Aye 9, No 0." Even more important, individual Christians, who had been living safe, protective, non-risk taking lives, discovered the power of committed action. More than literature, diatribes, workshops, study groups or classes, the direct observable acts of small groups of action oriented people are the leaven which infiltrates and redeems the life of the congregation.

Notes

1. Richard Schaull, *Heralds of a New Reformation*. Orbis, 1984, pp. 35-6.
2. Miranda, *Being*. pp. 108-9.
3. *Ibid*. p. 190.
4. Soelle, *Challenge*. pp. 7-10.

5

Ideological Issues and Biblical Faith

Thus far we have avoided any extended examination of theoretical questions. This is not primarily an academic analysis of libertion thought. It is rather a guide book for churches and their constituents in the affluent world, who are seeking to live in faithfulness to the will of God. It is basically about evangelism, and seeks to offer modalities of congregational praxis leading to our salvation; our being made whole; our liberation from those captivities which bind us.

However, certain ideological matters must be addressed if we are to act responsibly. This chapter deals with three of them:

1. The relationship between liberation theology and economic theories.
2. The relationship between liberation theology and spirituality.
3. The way in which liberation theology views Bible study.

For those whose knowledge of liberation theology comes from the secular press, news magazines or the pronouncements of fundamentalists, the matter is usually reduced to, "Well, it's just communism, isn't it?" Those who have no doubts about it probably haven't picked up this volume in the first place. We cannot speak to them or even with them. They know that anything of this sort is the work of the devil, at worst, or an anti-U.S. conspiracy, at best.

Many others have read the same materials and listened to reports of the Vatican's misgivings about how certain theologians are speaking and acting among the poor in Latin America, but believe there is another side to the story and are still searching for better answers. They may wonder if Latin American liberation movements are religious or only political in their genesis and orientation. They may be unclear as to why the government of the United States has condemned the regime in Nicaragua, for instance, knowing the Sadinista administration includes several priests. I recently heard a well-read theologian wonder out loud if liberation theology was only a matter "for guerrillas, with a gun in one hand and a copy of Marx in the other." Yet for most of these thoughtful people the door is not closed. They come with questions which deserve careful responses.

It is naive to assume that there is no relationship between liberation thought and Marxism. It may be helpful, therefore, to spell out briefly what that relationship is and how it functions. There are common threads in both liberation theology and the Marxist analysis of history. But they differ in important ways. For a full treatment of this theme the works of Jose Miranda are recommended, principally *Marx and the Bible*.

In its simplest form, Marxism assumes that all of life can be reduced to conflicts arising out of the control of wealth. The fancy phrase is "dialectical materialism." Marx believed that in the struggle between the workers and those who own the means of production, which includes the land, there can never be peace until labor, which produces everything of value, overcomes capital which allows owners to control not only what the workers produce, but the lives of the workers themselves. As we shall presently see, liberation theology also presupposes an absolute need for elemental economic and political justice. While a few have more than enough, most people live in wretched conditions. Liberationists insist there must be a more equitable way to distribute the resources of this earth.

But liberation theologians do not see that process happening in the way Marx envisioned it. They see God at work. They see justice to be a matter of the advent of a new Messianic era. They see themselves as advocates for those involved in God's project, whose work includes direct political action as well as spiritual formation. They believe it is the plan and will of God that the oppressed be set free from their captivity.

Even though Miranda is comfortable with much in the classical Marxist analysis, he summed up the difference between Marx and the biblical writers as follows: "Marx believes that dialectics [class conflict] will produce justice in the world, and the Bible believes that faith will produce justice in the world."[1] Miranda points out that in Marxism there is no God active in history or remotely concerned about justice, whereas in the Judeo-Christian system God is at the center of it all.

> We do not mean to conceal the abysmal difference between Marx and the biblical authors, a difference stemming from the fact that the latter believe in God and his intervention and Marx does not. It is God who curses the earth because of man, according to Gen. 3:17 (cf 8:21). It is the wrath of God which "gives men over" to the immanent cataract of injustice of which they have made themselves guilty, according to Rom. 1:28-32.[2]

Gustavo Gutierrez, the principal architect of liberation theology, is suspicious of that part of Marxist thought which tends to reduce the gospel to activism. Salvation is more than economic justice, although, according to Gutierrez, there can be no salvation without it. He writes that the danger exists in a theology too much aligned with Marxism so that "all energies would be poured out into scattered commitment and an unmitigated activism."[3]

While many liberationists use Marxism as a way to understand history, the significant difference is this—Marxism posits no value other than materialism. Liberation theology posits God and God's redeeming work in Jesus Christ as the center of history and the root of all meaning. Marxist analysis and Christian thought do come to some similar conclusions. Both understand that we live in a world choked by evil. Miranda describes the different routes taken to explain its cause:

> Marx and Paul coincide in their intuition of the totality of evil! Sin and injustice form an all-comprehensive

and all-pervasive organic structure. Paul calls this totality *kosmos*. Marx calls it "capitalism."[4]

Miranda argues that in both systems sin is the product of human decisions.

> In both Marx and the Bible the basis for all thought is this thesis which is the most revolutionary imaginable: Sin and evil are not inherent to humanity and history; they began one day through human work and they can, therefore, be eliminated.[5]

He quotes Romans 5:12, ". . . sin came into the world through one man. . . ."

For Marx the remedy is revolution—bloody, violent revolution—which is the inevitable result of the class struggle. For Christians the answer lies in the work, the death and resurrection of Jesus Christ, and in the project given the church by the Holy Spirit, which portends the establishment of God's sovereign rule over all things.

It is only fair to point out that liberationists, looking at the gospel and human existence through the eyes of the poor in the Third World, see capitalism as antithetical to the kingdom. Given their experience, in which wealthy oligarchies have dominated the lives of the masses by the control and ownership of the means of production, it is difficult to quarrel with their conclusion. Capitalism has been disastrous for the oppressed.

Leonardo Boff, one of the clearest advocates for the rights of the poor, put it this way:

> The principal contradiction of this "woeful system" [capitalism] lies in the fact that all, by their labor, contribute to the production of goods, but only certain ones—those who hold capital—acquire ownership of these goods, to the exclusion of others. . . . Radical criticism calls for a new form of organization for the whole of society, an organization on other bases—no longer from a point of departure of the capital held in the hands of a few, but an organization of society based on everyone's labor, with everyone sharing in the means and goods of production as well as in the means of power. And this is called liberation.[6]

If, therefore, liberationists hold misgivings about Marxism, the fundamental hermeneutic, [method of interpreting and understanding history], tends to be significantly influenced by a Marxist analysis.

Many in the United States believe capitalism has served the United States, and the world, well. Without capital formation and the free enterprise system, life would be more dismal for us. We believe that in a modified and humanized capitalism, or in a yet undefined third system, there may be hope for the wretched of the earth; a hope similarly promised by Marxism, but undeliverable in that system. Many liberationists call this line of thinking decadent liberalism. Yet it is an honest position many thoughtful Christians take, including the author of this book.

On the other hand, it is clear why Christians looking at the conditions of the masses in the Third World, conclude that capitalism, as practiced among them, is a consummate evil. If that is not our experience, it may be that as there are a variety of forms of socialism, there are a variety of forms of capitalism.

For example, in China, a society in which traditionally a few wealthy families held everyone else in economic subjugation and poverty; a socialism increasingly intertwined with free enterprise has not only held out hope, but has significantly improved life for those who had been oppressed. It may be that different societies call for different answers to their particular problems.

In China I learned not to label things too quickly. Calling something "communism" or "capitalism" may often be to put a tag on it which truncates, not enhances, communication. We were visiting a tea collective in a southeastern province. The collective is one unit of a larger commune, which is similar to what we would call a county. The central government, through the commune, sets production quotas for each collective farm.

We noticed a sizable modern hotel standing in the small village where members of the collective lived. We were informed that the hotel was for Chinese tourists—not foreign visitors—and was owned by the collective.

"Each collective has a quota of tea which must be produced," we were told. "But we can produce much more than our quota. We have our own label, and sell this excess tea on the open world market. The funds we received were used to build the hotel. Each family shares in the money which the operation of the hotel generates. It is possible to gain a larger interest in the hotel by buying the units owned by others. At the end of the year the committee which operates the hotel divides the money among all those who have units, depending on how many units they possess."

I quickly responded: "I understand the system. You have capital formation, investments, a corporation with a board of directors, management, shareholders, a stock exchange and profits. That's called 'capitalism.'"

The shock was immediate. "Oh no! It is socialism!" I always believed that if it looked like a cow, gave milk like a cow, mooed like a cow, it wasn't sensible to call it a giraffe. I am now more convinced that communication happens when we are more hesitant to put labels on things. Calling the economics espoused by liberationists "Marxism" may only inhibit dialogue. In fact, many believe that we stand on the edge of exciting new economic systems which defy all of our previously applicable labels.

If many among the poor of the world seem too quickly to have wed their cause to Marxism, the church in the developed world must bear much of the responsibility. Freedom is inevitable if we believe the biblical account. God stands with the oppressed, and God will ultimately triumph over sin and death. That is the message in the story of the Exodus, the vision of the prophets and the proclamation of Jesus. It is easy for those who are not oppressed to forget this main course in God's great banquet; to get caught up in our physical amenities and organizational busyness, and forget that all history is salvation history, the history of how God sets free.

Since history is instructive, we may observe just how Latin America became infected with communism. With the demise of colonial empires early in this century, the wretched of the earth discovered just as they no longer needed to live under the political domination of the major European powers, neither did they need to live in economic dependence.

With the decline of Spanish hegemony in Latin America, God provided the opportunity for something new to break out.

We must remember that long after Spain lost political control, she still controlled the church. Only in recent years have there been indigenous bishops. In the four centuries following the "Christianizaton" of Latin America, Catholic bishops were sent from the Iberian Peninsula. It is also well to remember that the wealth of the church and its religious power over people were combined with the political power of the despotic regimes, which rushed into the hiatus when the colonial powers were dethroned. Both church and state were kept in power by independent military establishments, which although not officially part of the governments, often decided what governments were to be in power.

That system began to collapse a generation ago. Among the major contributing factors to the breakdown of this trinity of tyranny was the change in the way the church began to exercise its role. Priests and religious workers became increasingly scarce. New spiritual currents, which did not carry with them the supersitious authority of the older established institutions, were beginning to run through Latin America. Vatican II, with its call for renewal, collegiality and social witness, moved the church quickly along that path, as did the rise of Catholic Action and the establishment of Christian Democratic Parties.

New bishops, many of whom were now being appointed from among the people, were beginning to take a closer look at the plight of the poor, and in 1955 established a permanent episcopal organization for consultation, study and action: The Latin American Episcopal Council (CELAM). This body not only interpreted the post Vactican II social encyclicals, but also produced impressive statements of its own at meetings held in Medellin, Colombia, in 1968, and in Puebla, Mexico, in 1979. The bishops were assisted by theologians who clustered around Gustavo Gutierrez, a Peruvian priest, whose foundational work, *A Theology of Liberation*, was published in 1971. Gutierrez was viewed with considerable suspicion by many of the conservative bishops, who had come from the old established families. Only after considerable in-fighting did his work on liberation become the theological core of the Puebla document and the subsequent work of CELAM.

Protestant churches also became aware of the plight of the poor and the political repression of the masses. In 1981 the Latin American Council of Churches (CLAI) met in Huampani, Peru, and took a stand similar to the position articulated in the Medellin and Puebla statements of the Catholic bishops.

The United States, its government, its business enterprises and its religious communities, were faced with a decision. Had the United States stood in solidarity with the "huddled masses yearning to be free," instead of with corporate interests, both national and multi-national, who were themselves in a league with the landed oligarchies, a different history might have been produced. But the United States did not see, or did not care to see, the nature of the problem. Instead of paying attention to an emerging Christian consciousness, these developments tended to be evaluated only by how they affected U.S. political and economic hegemony. The result was another effort to reinstitute the Monroe Doctrine. Scores of unholy marriages between corporate interests and the wealthy oligarchies were consumated. If their liaisons worked to the detriment of the peoples of these lands, little was said and less was done.

Early on in Cuba, our government supported Batista, and North Americans used Havana as a playground. But while the marginalization of the masses was being exacerbated by our policies and alliances, a new political movement was brewing in the hills far from Havana's slums and casinos. Not finding support from the United States, Fidel Castro turned to the only place which seemed ready to provide assistance, the Soviet Union. Similar stories can be told about other nations, including Chile, where the United States not only failed to support a democratically elected regime, but participated in the assassination of its President in a plot widely held to have been orchestrated by the CIA. In his place we backed a military junta, which made life for North American corporate interests much easier, and existence for the poor in Chile much more difficult.

In Nicaragua the United States' stubborn alliance with the despotic Somoza regime is largely responsible for the disaffection with which the Nicaraguan people now hold our country. One is forced to wonder whether the United States would be reaping the whirlwind in Latin America if the United States hadn't sown to the wind over the last generation. Had those of us who claim to be addressed by the biblical message been able to hear it, the world might be a safer, more gracious place for all.

The issues before your congregation, in relationship to the rest of the world, are religious and biblical, not fundamentally about economics and politics. For Christians, economics and politics are derivative of the gospel of freedom, not precedent to it. Our sin is that we allow our theology to grow out of our sociology and not the other way around. Congregations intent on faithfulness to God will begin with the biblical message as a commission to action and allow that commitment to inform every political and economic perspective.

The second theoretical matter to consider involves a perceived lack of spirituality among liberationists. Isn't this just a political religion, which is no religion at all? With all the talk about revolution, a new social order and politics, liberation theology sounds like no more than secularism dressed up in religious language.

In order to grasp the profundity of spiritual power in libertion theology we must look far beyond *TIME* magazine and turn to the theologians themselves. Their spirituality, however, is quite unlike the individual piety which often passes for spirituality in the United States. It is an aggressive, compelling, life changing and dramatically biblical encounter with the Spirit.

Henri Nouwen, one of the spiritual giants of our era, sets the tone when he writes in the introduction to a book on spirituality by Gutierrez, *We Drink from Our Own Wells*:

> The spirituality, as Gustavo articulates it, makes it impossible to reduce liberation theology to a political movement. The struggle to which the God of the Bible calls his people is much larger than a struggle for political or economic rights. It is a struggle against all the forces of death wherever they become manifest and a struggle for life in the fullest sense.[7]

A profound sense of the holy runs through the literature, sermons and work of liberationists. One cannot be in the presence of Dom Helder Camara without sensing magnificent spiritual power and authority, the same kind of presence those must have experienced who encountered St. Francis of Assisi, St. Teresa of Avila, Pascal or any of the spiritual giants of Christian history. It was never a detached spirituality they exhibited; never a disembodied other-worldliness, but a sense that life itself, in all its details, is a confrontation with the eternal; a direct involvement with the Spirit of God, which pervades and informs every aspect of life.

The profundity of the Mystery before which we bow seems particularly clear in those whose mission is lived out among the poorest of the poor. Can anyone possibly say they find a lack of spiritual content in the life and work of Mother Teresa, as she labors among the wretched of the earth in Calcutta, and pleads their case in the rest of the world? This godly woman is not usually thought of as a liberation theologian, but that is only because we forget that liberationism is orthopraxis, not orthodoxy.

Jesus' spirituality was most evident when he walked among the oppressed, not as a shadowy figure, but as the incarnation of mercy, grace and freedom. If the declaration of his mission at Nazareth and the parable of the last judgment are not spiritual declarations, then spirituality has been reduced to spiritualism, and spiritualism is a heresy. Spiritualism denies the incarnation. It reduces the Christian faith to speculation about some other world. Christian spirituality has always been about this world and its redemption by the power of the Spirit.

Boff writes: "At the roots of the theology of liberation we find a spirituality, a mysticism: the encounter of the poor with the Lord."[8] Gutierrez puts it this way:

> We need a vital attitude, all-embracing and synthesizing, informing the totality as well as every detail of our lives; we need a "spirituality." Spirituality, in the strict and profound sense of the word, is the dominion of the Spirit. If "the truth will set you free," (John 8:32) the Spirit "will guide you into all truth" (John 16:13) and will lead us to complete freedom, the freedom from everything that hinders us from fulfilling ourselves as men and sons of God, and the freedom to love and enter into communion with God and with

others; it will lead us along the path of liberation because "where the spirit of the Lord is, there is liberty" (2 Cor. 3:17).[9]

At the heart of the Christian gospel lies the incarnation: "And the word became flesh and dwelt among us, full of grace and truth; we have beheld his glory, glory as of the only Son from the Father" (John 1:14). Christian spirituality celebrates the presence of God in human history. For us he was made man. We have not a high priest in the heavens, but one who "emptied himself, taking the form of a servant" (Philippians 2:7). Ours is an incarnate faith as well as a faith in the incarnation.

The complaint that liberation theology is entirely too worldy, is only a modern recitation of the earliest Christian heresy. Listen to how the author of 2 John puts it: "For many deceivers have gone out into the world, men who will not acknowledge the coming of Jesus Christ in the flesh; such a one is the deceiver and the antichrist" (2 John 7).

Most of us have heard the whining lament: "Reverend, the church shouldn't be involved in politics. We ought to stick to spiritual matters and stay out of things that don't concern us." That is simply the latest way to articulate the docetic heresy, and should be dealt with—in pastoral love of course—just as did the writer of this little epistle to "the elect lady and her children." We call it what it is: a perversion of the gospel. Those who don't want their religion involved in the affairs of this world need to try some other religion. Christianity won't pass their test. We shall return to some practical examples in later chapters. Suffice to say now, the only profound spirituality the Bible knows anything about is an incarnational one. Jesus was not a disembodied ghost. The Holy Spirit did not prompt the apostles to retreat from the crucial problems facing the human family.

Hugo Echegaray reminds us that God did not come to us only or even principally through doctrinal statements by which some people hold special spiritual knowledge; that is called gnosticism and is the second oldest heresy in Christendom. "Jesus is the way, the truth and the life in his very person, in his words and action as an indivisible unity, in the real existence that he accepted in its totality as a gift."[10] Echegaray goes on to suggest that Jesus' adversaries denied that God had come into the world as Messiah, and by that refusal denied that his Messianic kingdom should become real in history. To deny the involvement of the church in the affairs of the world is to commit the same heretical error.

Leonardo Boff, who was best known in 1985 as the theologian whose writings prompted an appearance before the arbiters of orthodoxy in the Vatican, described the meaning of Christianity in the following carefully woven argument, which was first articulated by the Council of Chalcedon.

> In christological terms, to speak of Jesus as God in such a way that he is not human is monophysitism—the heresy that attributed only the divine nature to Jesus. To speak of him as a human being in a way as to imply that he is not God is Nestorianism—the heresy named for Nestorius, which asserted Jesus' humanity to the point of negating his divinity. . . . It is monophysitic to assert that there can be salvation without historical liberations . . . without an openness to salvation . . . salvation intrinsically includes historical liberations. Jesus, our salvation, is also our liberator: he conjoins salvation to liberation. Deeds and praxis not in themselves religious—healing, restoring sight to the blind and so on—are presented as concrete forms of the presence of the kingdom of God. . . . At the same time, salvation transcends every historical liberation, for death has not yet been vanquished: we have not yet come within God, nor have we been totally assumed by God, nor has all creation been transfigured.[11]

James Cone puts in practical terms the insistence that spiritual and political issues cannot be separated when he says:

> When the gospel is spiritualized so as to render invisible the important economic distinctions between the haves and the have-nots, the dialectical relationship between faith and the practice of political justice is also obscured.[12]

Gutierrez says:

> There is no aspect of human life that is unrelated to the following of Jesus. The road passes through every dimension of our existence. . . . A spirituality is not restricted to the so-called religious aspects of life: prayer and worship. It is not limited to one sector but is all embracing, because the whole of human life, personal and communal, is involved in the journey. A spirituality is a manner of life that gives us a profound unity to our prayer, thought and action.[13]

As I have often responded when rebuked by sincere people who think the church ought to stay out of politics, which usually means some vital matter which affects the human condition:

> Show me an issue in which God has not the slightest interest and I will stay away from it. But the matters you are talking about; war and peace, world hunger, oppression and injustice, are matters about which God is and always has been profoundly concerned. For us to be involved is simply faithfulness to the gospel; and to the Lord.

Liberation theology does not begin with doctrinal statements. Yet it is important within the life of the congregation to make clear that liberationism lies at the center of orthodoxy. Those who deny the involvement of the Spirit in this world in all its dimensions are not only on the edge of orthodox Christian thought, but some distance beyond that edge.

The third ideological question concerns how theological reflection, Bible study and other academic disciplines are viewed by liberation theology, and how they shape Christian praxis. At this point, liberation theologians maintain a healthy suspicion about the academic enterprise in general, and the historical-critical way in which the academic world goes about Bible study in particular.

If traditional scholarship is committed to the scientific method of inquiry, liberation theology starts from quite another perspective. It makes the assumption, a priori, that the initial Christian commitment is to liberation. This affirmation comes early in the game. One does not study the Bible to ascertain whether or not it is true. Liberation theology begins with commitment, not with reflection. Reflection grows out of commitment, not the other way around. The basic interpretative tool, or hermeneutic, is the commitment itself.

It is axiomatic that in the chronology of history God's action preceded any human reflection on it, let alone any oral tradition or written document about it. God's activity comes first, and a record of it is produced later. Liberation theologians tend to see traditional Western scholarship as scientific research and analysis without the fire of prior commitment, and therefore as dilettantism.

Shubert Ogden describes the classical historical-critical method as being one of two sorts:

> Christian theology is formally characterized as either the process or the product of a certain kind of critical reflection. As a *process* of reflection . . . insofar as it involves any prior commitment, it is committed simply to understanding the meaning of the Christian witness and to assessing its truth, and, therefore, to any and all human being insofar as, being human, they are somehow moved by the question of the ultimate meaning of their existence to which this witness presents itself as the answer. As a *product* of this kind of reflection, by contrast, theology is constituted as such, not by a question, but by an answer—specifically, by a reasoned answer to the question of the meaning of Christian witness. . . . As such, therefore, it is once again, a commitment to any and all human beings, insofar as, being human, they not only ask about the ultimate meaning of their existence, but are also bound to seek only the truth in doing so.[14]

If Ogden is certain both approaches eventuate in commitment to the truth, liberationists are not so sure. They view theological reflection and Bible study not as academic exercises, but as responses to the God who has already acted in history, and who calls out a people in the Christian era to celebrate the advent of the Messianic age.

Liberation theologians are disinterested in Bible study, or other academic enterprises, which are no more than a scientific inquiry into this or that bit of evidence or historical curiosity. It is not that they believe scholarly inquiry is improper, only of limited usefulness. They maintain that God is known not by what God thought but by what God did. To know God is not to know about God. To know God is to do justice. It is in doing the truth one is encountered by the Holy.

The theological task is to incarnate the freedom of God and the freedom God has willed for the human family. Liberationists insist that it is not the lack of knowledge of the gospel, or even the lack of belief which stymies the enterprise of the kingdom, but the lack of liberating praxis by those most knowledgeable. The task of theological reflection is to formulate the gospel message so as to provide the incentive for liberation, not to provide interesting or even helpful information.

Liberation theologians look with considerable despair on what goes on in most seminaries, divinity schools and departments of religious studies. They do not see that it leads to action. Bible study among the poor, however, not weighed down with academic tools, can be and in fact is, more direct and life changing. Bible study in the base communities proceeds from the plight of the poor and leads to liberating praxis. The question among them is not, "What is the nature of God's project for us?" but, "How shall we engage in it?" The decision to engage has already been made.

In describing the results when liberationists overcame the hiatus between theory and practice, which seemed to smother most North American and European centers of learning, Lee Cormie writes:

> No longer could political action for social justice be considered secondary to the spiritual dimensions of faith.... No longer could theory, even in theology, be divorced from action, and thus the emphasis on praxis.... No longer could the Bible be interpreted through the eyes of the discrete, autonomous, "rational" individual of liberal thought, and thus the emphasis on the collective dimensions of salvation and on the biblical faith in doing justice.[15]

Obviously those interested in the freedom of the oppressed, and the liberation of the oppressors from our oppressiveness, are not going to throw out critical reflective methods of doing theology and Bible study. Religious theoreticians and scientists, and the scholarly work they produce, will remain vital to the religious enterprise and to the work of Christ. Nevertheless, what the liberationists have to say ought to modify and inform ways we do theological and biblical studies, not only in the academic world, but also in our churches.

How does this question affect the nature of Bible study in your congregation? Perhaps nowhere in all of church life do we have a more blemished record. Classes of the "saints" meet Sunday after Sunday, decade after decade, jumping up and down on ten verses a week, covering the Bible over and over again, and manage to come out of that life-long process just about where they went into it, without any serious commitment to the heralding of the kingdom or the liberation of those in chains.

In our more sophisticated congregations, among an intellectual elite, we might even expound on the synoptic problem, the case for Third Isaiah, or the relationship between the symbolism in the book of Job and the religious traditions of Persia. But to what end? Is anyone's life or commitment seriously affected one way or the other? Does liberation take place, the Messianic age evidenced, the good news of salvation in Christ incarnated? Does Bible study lead to liberation for either the students or for others? Is there any connection between the study of the healing miracles of Jesus and healing for anybody? Liberationists suggest we begin with commitment, with a declaration of God's liberating purpose in history, and allow the study of the Bible to flow from that affirmation.

What if we assume the Bible is the record of God's passion to free the oppressed, and a description of how God intervened in history to that end? And what if we further assume that the Bible provides us the methodology whereby we join with God in this liberating work? How does that alter the way we do Bible study in our congregations? What if we go even further and assume with Jose Miranda that the basic purpose of religion is to bring salvation to the suffering and oppressed?

> A god who intervenes in history to elicit religious adoration of himself and not to undo the hell of

cruelty and death that human history has become is an immoral god in the deepest sense of the word. A god who is reconciled or merely indifferent to the pain of human beings is a merciless god, a monster, not the ethical God whom the Bible knows. . . . Equally immoral is the god for whom the end of injustice and innocent suffering is a secondary or subordinate imperative.[16]

For faithful members of our congregation the Bible remains a closed, useless book, because few see in it a manual of arms in the struggle against oppression, disease and all the specific captivities of those who study it. If the prior assumption is made that it describes ways in which we share with God in the liberating enterprise, and we study it not to master its critical problems but to equip ourselves for engagement with the world, then Bible study might be the most exciting thing the congregation does. I am not suggesting we throw out our commentaries, but that rather alongside our systematic, scientific, historical-critical methodology, we learn from liberation theology—but initially from the Bible itself—that it is first of all a handbook on the praxis of liberation.

Notes

1. Miranda, *Marx and.* p. 202.
2. *Ibid.* p. 278.
3. Gutierrez, *We Drink.* p. 129.
4. Miranda, *Marx and.* p. 250.
5. *Ibid.* p. 277.
6. Boff, *Salvation.* p. 8.
7. Gutierrez, *We Drink.* p. xvi.
8. Boff, *Salvation.* p. 2.
9. Gutierrez, *A Theology.* pp. 203-4.
10. Echegaray, *The Practice.* p. 9.
11. Boff, *A Salvation.* pp. 58-9.
12. James Cone, *Challenge.* p. 54.
13. Gutierrez, *We Drink.* p. 88.
14. Shubert Ogden, *Challenge.* pp. 131-2.
15. Lee Cormie, *Challenge.* p. 27.
16. Miranda, *Being.* p. 187.

6

Liberation Theology and Political Action

We now move from an analysis of theoretical problems to how congregations address specific issues posed by liberation theology. Once confronted by the God who speaks through those who are marginalized, it is our task, our project, to shape a course of action and be about it. We begin with the most problematic and difficult step of all—the involvement of the church in politics. In the United States there would appear to be a practical impediment. Written into our psyches, as well as our Constitution, is the separation of church and state. "Congress shall make no law regarding the establishment of a religion, or prohibiting the free exercise thereof."

Churches have been wary of supporting candidates or becoming aligned with parties. No minister can get in hot water more quickly than by urging from the pulpit, the election of a certain candidate or party. In many places in the world that is perfectly natural, but since this book is addressed principally to a U.S. audience, we need to maintain a sense of realism not only about what is appropriate, but also about what is possible. Yet, even with our cultural and constitutional sanctions, we can never say never. On occasion, faithfulness to the gospel means political activity. If the Constitution mandates a separation of church and state, the gospel mandates a direct relationship between religion and public policy.

It is too easy to sidestep the painful problems by suggesting the appropriateness of taking a position on issues but not on candidates or parties. Often that is a convenient way to avoid the necessary clarity integral to the shaping of public policy. We live in a time when policies are determined by taking polls. Candidates and parties attempt to position themselves as close to the middle of the road as possible, leaning only slightly this way or that. Defining where the center is has become a high art.

Electoral politics is played between the 40-yard lines. No party, which strays beyond the constraining boundaries of "the U.S. consensus" is likely to win elections. It is often difficult to discover just where the major parties differ on the big issues. As election day draws closer, politicians tend to sound more and more like each other in terms of how they talk about the issues, while simultaneously trying to demonstrate how they provide a clear alternative. In a tweedle-dee and tweedle-dum political environment it is inane for the church to come down on one side or the other.

Often we can help clarify the issues by moving beyond the safe territory between the 40-yard lines, to a position which takes account of God's radical liberating will. Discourse which lies outside the great U.S. consensus has its limitations. But that is where the will of God is often found. Political dialogue, however, is only a first step, and is bedeviled with bogs of rhetorical quicksand.

During the late 60s and 70s, in a time of frantic political activity on college campuses, I served a parish at the University of Chicago. We provided a forum for a dozen political groups which held interminable discussions about who was the most ideologically pure. "I am lefter than thou," rang through the halls. When it came to making any significant contribution to ending the war, these groups of constricted ideologists were almost useless. All their energy was consumed in posturing. It reminded me of body building exhibitions in which contestants engage in outrageous contortions in order to impress a jury that their muscular development is worthy of the blue ribbon. Liberation theology suggests direct action as more productive of social change than is discourse.

Liberationism moves us from rhetoric, charity and even social service to direct political action. Many years ago I heard the statement: "Give a man a fish and you feed him for a day. Teach a man to fish and you feed him for a lifetime." The affirmation is true as far as it goes, for it runs the gamut of Christian praxis all the way from A to B. It is obviously true that simple acts of charity are vital. The first response to a hungry woman and her child is to get them something to eat, right then and right there. Most communities these days operate soup kitchens. The one in our city, staffed by members of our churches, is called "The Open Door." It provides a free, nutritious, hot meal for anyone who shows up. Several hundred meals are served each day. There are no questions asked, no means tests, no requirement to attend a religious service. It is one of the many acts of simple human compassion Christians are called to perform.

If "The Open Door" gives a man a fish, it does not solve his problem beyond that day. Tomorrow he is hungry again. We discover that good works cannot stop at good deeds. We move, therefore, to social services, which begin to have political implications. Providing food stamps and Aid to Dependent Children is not exactly teaching a family how to fish. It is, rather, seeing that they get their daily fish in a systematic and socially authorized way. It is charity which begins to move toward justice. It relies on a political right, not on someone's good will—a fragile commodity.

Increasingly, however, evidences appear that the war on poverty, which generated many of these social welfare programs, failed to address the fundamental problems. The real need was to develop a system which provided a greater degree of self-sufficiency for those who were the objects of our collective good deeds. Instead of offering a daily fish, even on a regular basis, we looked for ways to teach people to fish. We produced job training programs, for instance. It was better to find regular employment for the recipients of the daily offerings of "The Open Door." Charity is, after all, degrading. It is not quite as degrading, so the argument went, when it has the official and somewhat anonymous stamp of government largess. Nevertheless, one only occasionally encounters an individual who would rather line up for food stamps than be engaged in productive work. At least that was the popular wisdom among liberals. The assumption was made among conservatives, who took a dim view of charity at the public trough, that most of those who were the objects of these "give them a daily fish" subsidies were able-bodied men and women perfectly capable of getting and holding jobs.

Evidence to the contrary poured in. We discovered we were dealing with large numbers of small children, the elderly, feeble, afflicted, limited and unemployable. We also discovered that no matter how many training programs one devised, the U.S. economic system maintained a steady level of unemployment of 6 to 12 percent. In some places and among some populations the rate was much higher. It rose to, and remained at, 25 percent among black teenagers.

A similar progression of events and insights evolved in our relationship to the Third World. Food handouts were replaced by agricultural programs. As noble as that move seemed to be, we all too often cast our "teach them to fish" lot with developmentalists. In chapter two we discussed how development often accrued huge benefits to those providing the tools, as well as to a limited number of wealthy individuals and families in the developing nations. If teaching people to fish meant they were forced to abandon the production of food crops in favor of the production of cash crops, who benefitted? We might have satisfied our consciences, believing we had done the noble thing, when we had only succeeded in further marginalizing large populations.

What we learn, as we sit at the feet of the poor, is that the people we thought we were teaching to fish weren't near the river. We might have provided them the latest Garcia rods and reels, superior nylon nets and the finest lures, but we allowed, indeed we participated in the building of enormous barbed wire fences which insured that the masses of people could not get to the water.

The poor have taught us that the basic problem is structural, not technical or educational. It is the political system which denies access to the river. If the marginalized were to be set free, the barbed wire had to come down. All our righteous good deeds could become good works only when there was a restructuring of the political systems which determined who could fish and who could not. To be committed to the poor, therefore, means to be committed to political reformation.

But even when the need for direct political involvement became clear, we were often hesitant because of the low regard in which politics is held. We think it to be a dirty business. Demonstrations of the validity of this assumption abound! Liberationists also harbor a sturdy suspicion of politics in the Third World; but you know it is the only game in town. You either play it, or you allow yourselves to be victimized by those who play hard, while convincing you the contest is outside the proper bounds of religion.

Consider the following affirmations from the Puebla text:

> Far from despising political activity, the Christian faith values it and holds it in high esteem. . . . The need for the church's presence in the political arena flows from the very core of the Christian faith. . . . Politics, "in the broad sense," of seeking "the common good on both the national and international plane." . . . Its task is to spell out the fundamental values of every community . . . reconciling equality with freedom, public authority with the legitimate autonomy and participation of individual persons and groups . . . [Politics] is a way of paying worship to the one and only God.[1]

The Christian engages in political activity, knowing it is a proximate and dangerous endeavor. It is most dangerous, however, when we engage in it quite unaware we are doing so. To identify the status-quo, no matter how oppressive, with the will of God, or to pretend indifference, is to fall into a clever political trap. Even while declaring that political activity may be a means of grace, Puebla offers a stern caveat lest the church become caught in schemes generated by political self-interest.

> Manipulation of the church, always a risk in political life, [is present when] priests and religious . . . proclaim a gospel devoid of economic, social, cultural, and political implications. In practice this mutilation comes down to a kind of complicity with the established order, however unwitting.[2]

One only has to recall the infamous role played by the court sanctioned prophets of the king in the Old Testament. Every generation has its collection of religious leaders perfectly willing to sit at the king's table, eat the king's food, laugh at the king's jokes and agree with whatever the king says. The church in Latin America has been captive of the principalities and power with which it has shared social and economic oversight.

Leonardo Boff sees the relationship between the church and the political establishment to be a central challenge of liberation theology. He writes: "This is the key question . . . How may we see the presence of God, and God's grace—or the presence of the evil one, and sin—within economic and social processes?"[3] Boff assumes that in every age and in every place Christians must understand the potential for evil in human systems, but at the same time engage them in vigorous debate about human freedom, because they always provide a barrier which must be penetrated for the sake of the good.

Gutierrez calls to account as being unfaithful to the gospel Christians or Christian institutions who say "politics is none of our business." He writes: "Any claim to noninvolvement in politics . . . is nothing but a subterfuge to keep things as they are. The mission of the Church cannot be defined in the abstract."[4]

Desmond Tutu insists that those who parrot the cry, "Don't mix religion and politics" do so because they don't want anything to change. They tend to favor whatever establishment is in power, no matter how tyrannical or unjust. Politicians will utter the cry when they do not want the ethical demands inherent in faith to interfere with the injustices they wish to perpetuate. In a taped message to the All African Church Conference held in Nairobi, a conference the Bishop was unable to attend because the government had taken away his passport, he declared:

> If the church demonstrates a concern for the victims of neglect or exploitation or denounces the widening gap in the country between the very few who are rich and the vast majority who are poor . . . then the church will be accused of meddling in affairs it knows very little about. This kind of criticism will reach crescendo proportions if the church not merely provides an ameliorative ambulance service, but aims to expose the root causes; if it becomes radical . . . then it will arouse the

wrath of those who benefit from the particular inequitable status quo.⁵

When the church is in the vest pocket of the political establishment, its relationship to the poor is reduced either to offering the despots religious sanction for their oppressiveness, or to acting as the paternalistic arm of the regime. It reaches out to the marginalized, but usually in the form of offering state sponsored charity. It comes to the aid of the poor, but it says nothing about the inequitable systems which keep them poor. It provides just enough help to take the edge off the hunger which is a prerequisite to the struggle for liberation. The church in these cases becomes a courtesan. And when you eat at the king's table you do not comment in public about the king's table manners.

The prophetic tradition of the Bible offers an alternative to these passive responses to despotism. Kings have a way of ignoring the prophets who privately attempt to offer guidance. Either the prophet quietly retreats or goes public. The Old Testament is replete with stories of prophets going public. Consider what Jeremiah had to say in a passage often cited by liberation theologians.

> Woe to him who builds his house by unrighteousness,
>   and his upper room by injustice;
> who makes his neighbor serve him for nothing,
>   and does not give him his wages;
> who says, "I will build myself a great house,
>   with spacious upper rooms"
>   and cuts out windows for it,
>   paneling it with cedar,
>   and painting it with vermillion.
> Do you think you are a king
>   because you compete in cedar?
> Did not your father eat and drink
>   and do justice and righteousness?
>   Then it was well with him.
> He judged the cause of the poor and needy;
>   then it was well.
> Is not this to know me?
>   says the LORD.

> But you have eyes and heart
>   only for your dishonest gain,
> for shedding innocent blood,
>   and for practicing oppression and violence.
> Therefore thus says the Lord concerning Jehoiakim the son of Josiah king of Judah:
> "They shall not lament for him
>   saying,
> 'Ah my brother!' or 'Ah sister!'
> They shall not lament for him
>   saying,
> 'Ah lord!' or 'Ah his majesty!'
> With the burial of an ass he shall be buried,
> dragged and cast forth beyond the
>   gates of Jerusalem" (Jeremiah 22:13-19).

Jurgen Kegler, a European liberationist reflects:

> These words are an open declaration of war on the king. They also show that Jeremiah takes sides. A king who does not support the cause of the wretched and the poor but instead creates wretchedness and poverty by his manner and his government violates the express will of God. This kind of public criticism, which calls into question the entire way of life in which the king exercised power, could not but meet with resistance from the kings.[6]

Politics is rarely neutral. By its very nature it is confrontational. Sides are taken. What one often hears from First World pulpits is advice for people to get out and vote, and a blessing on the process itself, regardless of the results of a particular struggle. It hardly occurs to us that the majority may be wrong, misled or unfaithful to the demands of God. Even properly elected governments can be despotic. The voice of the people is not necessarily the voice of God. But at an even more elemental level, the political claims of parties and candidates may not equally reflect the will of God.

Christians are called upon to make judgments between right and wrong. That is the risky but necessary condition of discipleship. To engage in the political struggle may mean having to tell the king what Jeremiah told Johoiakim. Engaging in politics in general, without interpreting the ethical and moral implications of particular political positions and the candidates who hold them, is like being in favor of the flag, apple pie and motherhood.

If we hesitate to be politically involved, the Bible is clear that God was not. God took sides! The story of the Exodus is the story of a political struggle. The liberation of the Hebrews took place in the midst of an active contest between opposing points of view on public policy; the point of view of the powerful, and the point of view of the powerless. God chose a politician named Moses to lead the opposition to the policies of the government. The covenant between God and the people could only be developed after the political matter was settled.

Gutierrez puts it this way:

> The God of the Exodus is the God of history and of political liberation more than he is the God of nature. ... Yahweh is the Liberator. ... The Covenant gives full meaning to the liberation from Egypt; one makes no sense without the other. The Covenant was an historical event ... which occurred in a moment of disruption, in an atmosphere of liberation; the revolutionary climate still prevailed: an intense spiritual impulse would arise from it, as often happens in history.[7]

The story of God's political involvement does not end with the Exodus, and is not replaced by the covenant and the Law. The rest of the Old Testament can be read as a record of God's relationship to and participation in the politics of Israel, as well as the nations Israel encountered. The involvement goes far beyond the "Thus says the Lord," uttered by the prophets. The words and work of Jeremiah, Amos and the other voices for righteousness, north and south, do not exhaust the evidence that God was vitally concerned with public policy and its execution. The chroniclers of Israel and Judah provide running commentaries on God's political preferences. Each successive king is graded on whether he did evil or good in the sight of the Lord. In the books of history, as well as the books of prophesy, we have evidence of God's political loyalties and activities.

The Old Testament is not always seen as a political document because we have not examined it with that overlay. We all come to the Bible with a particular set of interpretive tools. When an overhead projector is used in teaching, the lecturer may start with a basic graph, chart, outline or map. The meaning of that initial document does not come clear, however, until another transparency is placed over the first. The original document is interpreted by the imposition of the overlay. One can highlight a variety of factors depending on the overlay used. One may start with a simple outline of the United States, for instance, and then show rivers, mountains, state boundaries or the distribution of agricultural products, by means of the appropriate overlay.

Liberation theology suggests that in the study of the Scriptures it is helpful to use a somewhat different set of overlays than one finds in the typical congregational Bible study group, or in theological seminaries for that matter. If, for instance, we look at the basic document by asking the question: "In what ways was God involved in the political and civic life of the people? we suggest a different question. We do not alter the text or its message. All we have done is see the message from a fresh perspective.

If we place yet another transparency over the first, in which we ask: "In what ways did God's political preferences and involvement affect questions of justice for the oppressed?" we will have discovered yet another layer of biblical insight. An additional overlay can demonstrate how God demanded obedience in terms of right action, rarely in terms of right doctrine.

We now move the question of biblical study from information to praxis as we ask the final question: "How do we act in our day on behalf of the oppressed so that we are faithful to the God of the Bible?" We have now returned to a constant theme of this book, and of liberation thought: the need for a style of Bible study flowing from a preferential option for the poor which is rooted in action.

Bible study within the congregation, which uses a carefully designed set of critical overlays, may be the first step in addressing the political project God has given the church in our day. It is the church's task not only to declare but also to produce the fruits of the Messianic age, and the biblical record seen through a liberating hermeneutic is the initial key to that task.

Seeing the Bible as a series of ten verse sections, which provide hints for happy living; or even using classical critical tools, may be fruitless in an age whose central religious theme must be the liberation of the oppressed. For us the Bible must become the record of the relationship between God and the political systems under which people live. It mandates justice. It says that to know God is, in fact, to do justice. It is never satisfied until oppression and captivity are overtaken by the kingdom. God continually takes a political position. Nor does the Bible, at least the Old Testament, spend much time dealing with personal morality or even the forgiveness of individual sins. We only read that into it when we use an inaccurate, distorted or incomplete overlay.

Langdon Gilkey asserts that the entire Old Testament is a document mandating human freedom.

> The Old Testament [calls for] political liberation. This is not . . . a liberation from sin . . . it is a liberation from the dire consequences of sin, from the fate which sin continually creates and recreates for others in and through objective social structures. . . . Such change will reduce the scope and so the scourge of sin, and it will liberate sufferers from some of the consequences of sin.[8]

The chances, however, are remote that many congregations will become directly involved in the political life in the way godly men and women of the Old Testament were. It may be more helpful, therefore, to turn to the ministry of Jesus for clues as to how we may work on behalf of the oppressed within our political structures.

It is doubtful the argument will ever be settled as to whether or not Jesus supported the Zealots, a revolutionary party intent on overthrowing the Romans. The weight of the evidence indicates that Jesus held himself at some distance from the party. He refused the apparent offer to be the pointman in their effort to secure Jewish freedom through a violent assault on Roman rule. Gutierrez suggests it was not that Jesus disagreed with the Zealots about the need for freedom, nor even the methods necessary to achieve it, but that they represented far too narrow a nationalism. Jesus' mission was universal. The kingdom he advocated and whose coming he declared, knew no national boundaries.

At that same time Jesus was clearly preoccupied with issues of justice and liberation. It was this perspective, which looked much like the posture assumed by the Zealots, that may have led to his death at the hands of the political authorities, the oppressors of the Jewish people. It was the Roman custom to post on the cross the crime committed by the one being executed. The title affixed to Jesus' cross indicated that he was a political criminal. "King of the Jews," it read. The people were called to observe what happened to anyone who would challenge the domination of Caesar. According to the authorities, that is exactly what he had done.

Gutierrez points out that not only the Romans, but the leaders of the Jews, were wary of him on political grounds.

> The Sanhedrin had religious reasons for condemning a man who claimed to be the Son of God, but it also had political reasons: the teaching of Jesus, and his influence over the people challenged the privilege and power of the Jewish leaders. These political considerations were related to another which affected Roman authority itself; the claim to be Messiah and King of the Jews.... The trial of Jesus was a *political* trial and he was condemned for being a Zealot.[9]

If legitimate questions can be raised about the direct involvement of Jesus with a revolutionary party, there is no question that his teachings had political implications. The affirmation that he had come to herald a new kingdom cannot be seen apart from its political consequences. If there was to be a new Messianic age, with new standards, new ways of social organization, new ethical demands—that is laws—what was to happen to the authority of those then in power? The simple announcment that there was already present a system of social organization, whose public policies differed radically from the prevailing system, could only be interpreted as a political challenge.

The parables of the kingdom talk about public policy in which all the traditional ways of doing things are turned upside down. Class distinctions are over. People are paid according to their need, not according to their work; much to the consternation of those who had worked all day and gotten the same wage as those who worked only the last hour. Throughout his teachings the wealthy, influential and powerful came in for a bad time.

If there is no apparent political party with which Jesus aligns himself, there is a revolutionary political platform clearly out of harmony with what is going on at the time. Acts and words which call for a reordering of society on behalf of the oppressed are political acts and words! Acts of liberation always represent a political threat to the ruling classes.

As Jesus' teachings heralded a new social order, his mighty acts, healings, feeding the multitudes, receiving the least respected as "first in the kingdom," were signs that the new age was already present in the midst of an oppressive society. This new age, however, would not come with the massive political challenge common when one social system is overtaken by another. Its way of working was, in fact, subversive; like yeast, which is hidden in a corner of the dough but which inevitably infiltrates and changes the entire loaf. It is like an inconspicuous mustard seed, which once planted, becomes a mighty bush.

If the revolutionary activity, which seems to be integral to liberationism, is beyond where most First World Christians believe their churches should go, the life and teachings of Jesus suggest an alternative: the sort of involvement on behalf of the poor which informs, challenges and finally alters the political realities, like leaven in the lump.

This route raises the possibility that liberation theology may help us affirm and celebrate ways in which many "liberal" churches have traditionally worked. We suggest that possibility knowing it is anathema to most liberation theologians. Yet the abolition of slavery, reform of working conditions for children and all workers, eventually, civil rights, the rights of women, peace and disarmament and a host of other leavening movements have been acts of religious people operating in a political environment.

In the encyclical *Popularum Progressio*, Pope Paul VI speaks of building a world where "every man, no matter what his race, religion or nationality, can live a fully human life, freed from servitude imposed on him by other men or by national forces over which he had not sufficient control (section 47). The Pontif saw this cultural renewal as yeast-like, not as a revolutionary assault on the reigning political structures.

Our political work on behalf of the oppressed thus takes on a continuity with the whole church. It is not that we want to downplay the new insights and revolutionary ways of operating which are the gifts of liberation thought, replacing them with tired, moribund and useless liberal rhetoric. Yet, with all its defects and sinfulness, the church has not been devoid of a witness to the liberating presence of God in history, nor to the saving gospel of Jesus Christ. Its need for conversion is clear. But so is its long history of proclaiming the kingdom. While liberation thought suggests new levels of action which are considerably beyond where we have traditionally dared to venture, they are not so far beyond that we cannot see them from where we are.

We are coming to a crisis point, not only in North America, but also in the rest of the developed world, which will thrust us toward novel styles of political activity we have yet to fully define. At this writing the United States seems to be going through a political period in which less attention is being paid to the legitimate aspirations of the oppressed, and more paid to the prequisites of the rich. Humanizing efforts are being curtailed. Programs for the least advantaged and most marginalized are being seriously eroded. They are called welfare and dismissed as an inappropriate use of tax dollars. Programs for the wealthy, particularly within the business community, are called incentives or subsidies and held sacrosanct.

While the problem at home is evidenced in an increase in the number of unemployed, as well as the abandonment of other marginalized people, our policies toward the rest of the world continue to take an even more discouraging direction. In the name of national security, we negotiate "mutually beneficial" pacts with dictatorships of the worst sort, including the regimes in South Africa and South Korea. At the same time we escalate our threats, and in some cases bring actual military pressure on those nations seeking fresh avenues to address problems of massive poverty. Of course, our fear, particularly in this hemisphere, is the rise of communism. But the enemy has been misidentified. Communism is the result, not the cause, of human misery. And human misery cannot be overcome with tanks.

If we are called to be one people of God the whole world round—an elemental article of faith—then Christians in any nation must allow that universal loyalty to take precedence over every national loyalty. Herein lies one of the most difficult lessons of the gospel; a lesson most people have not learned, either in our time or at any time in Christian history.

The mutiplex ramifications of this set of problems will not be solved by study groups, committee meetings or prayer societies, each of which has an important place within the life of the church. The remedies to the grave problems we face are political.

I was recently present at an address given by a representative of one of England's outstanding international relief agencies. This group has come to the aid of the wretched of the earth, the starving and the dispossessed. Without what they have done, both in providing food on the spot and offering seed grains together with better agricultural techniques, thousands of people would have starved to death. I support the work of similar organizations verbally and financially.

Part of the presentation was a filmstrip featuring the organization's work in Ethiopia, which at that time was the focus of starvation in the world. The narrator declared that there had actually been an increase in the productive capacity of the agricultural regions of that nation since the inception of the famine. The problem was, he pointed out, that the land was being used for the production of coffee, tea and other cash crops, and not for the production of food.

During the question period I inquired as to what his agency was doing about the larger political issues it had identified. It was obvious by the answer that political matters were far beyond the scope of this particular agency, and indeed possibly beyond the scope of any arm of the church. These matter were, after all, political.

Unless we can be content with world starvation, and allow the root issues to be dismissed as *political*, about which we have nothing to say, the inevitable result will be other Marxist revolutions, preceded by an increase in human misery. More and more military strength on the part of the First World nations will then be called for to meet the new Marxist challenge. The end product can only be disastrous for everyone. The hope is that somehow, beginning with the poor themselves, but also penetrating our middle-class congregations, Christians will see that human survival, even the survival of one human, is a spiritual problem. Survival is, however, the kind of spiritual problem which must be addressed politically.

Liberation theology points the way by witnessing to the power of the gospel to make whole the lives of marginalized people, thus safeguarding the lives of all. This gift comes to us because the poor, and their advocates, understand they cannot avoid participation in the political solutions to human problems; and neither can we. If in the first instance the message is from the poor to the poor, we have been given the gift of overhearing the gospel as they articulate it. Observe what the Ecumenical Committee of the Churches of Peru says:

> As we see it, a perhaps faulty presentation of the Christian message may have given the impression that religion is indeed the opiate of the people. And we would be guilty of betraying the cause of Peru's development if we did not stress the fact that the doctrinal riches of the gospel contain a revolutionary thrust. Indeed the "God whom we know in the Bible is a liberating God, a God who destroys myths and alienations, a God who intervenes in history in order to break down the structures of injustice, and who raises up prophets in order to point out the way of justice and mercy. He is the God who liberates slaves (Exodus), who causes empires to fall and raises up the oppressed."[10]

Gutierrez comments: "It is then to the oppressed that the Church should address itself and not so much to the oppressors; furthermore, this action will give true meaning to the Church's witness to poverty."[11]

Many of the poor, and those who speak on their behalf, realize they engage in political activity at considerable personal risk. Just a few days before he was assassinated, Oscar Romero, Archbishop of El Salvador, said:

> If they kill me, I will rise again in the Salvadoran people. . . . If those Salvadorans who threaten to assassinate me should go so far as to carry out their

threats, I want you to know that I now offer my blood to God for justice and the resurrection of El Salvador. ... If God accepts the sacrifice of my life ... our hopes will soon become a reality.[12]

We close this chapter with the reiteration of a caveat. Even though we cannot escape the political dimensions of the kingdom, in the last analysis the kingdom is not a political reality. Its scope is far broader than setting in place the proper social system, as important as that is. Listen to how Leonardo Boff puts it:

> He is indeed the Messiah-Christ, but not one of a political nature. His kingdom cannot be particularized and reduced to a part of reality, such as politics. He came to heal all reality in all its dimensions, cosmic, human, social. The great drama of the life of Christ was to try to take the ideological content out of the word "kingdom of God" and make the people and his disciples comprehend that he signified something much more profound, namely, that he demands a conversion of persons and a radical transformation of the human world; that he demands a love of friends and enemies alike and the overcoming of all elements inimical to God and humankind.[13]

Notes

1. Boff, *Salvation*. p. 37.
2. *Ibid.* p. 38.
3. *Ibid.* p. 47.
4. Gutierrez, *A Theology*. p. 266.
5. Desmond Tutu, *Hope and Suffering*, Fount Paperbacks, pp. 36-7.
6. Jurgen Kegler, *God of the Lowly*, Orbis, 1984. p. 49.
7. Gutierrez, *A Theology*. p. 157.
8. Gilkey, *Challenge*. pp. 121-2.
9. Gutierrez, *A Theology*. p. 229.
10. *Ibid.* p. 116.
11. *Ibid.* p. 116.
12. Shaull, *Heralds*. p. 51.
13. Emilo Castro, *Sent Free*, Risk Books, 1985, p. 59.

7

The Question of Violence

Another profoundly difficult issue which arises as people from middle-class churches attempt to understand and use the insights of liberation theology is the question of violence. In this chapter we will first examine the violence which seems inherent in revolution. This is increasingly a route contemplated, if not employed, by the oppressed. And we'll examine the ethical problems this poses for those of us who tend to see the gospel through nonviolent eyes. How do we, in our First World congregations, engage in political action on behalf of the oppressed if they employ methods which violate our understanding of the gospel? We will then turn to the captivity which immobilizes and smothers us, the policies and practices of the First World, whose existence is rooted in violence and the threat of violence.

Many otherwise sympathetic persons in our congregations are blocked from understanding and appreciating liberation movements in the Third World because they immediately presuppose the violent nature of these struggles for freedom. It is assumed that revolution intrinsically connotes armed conflict, sabotage, assassinations and the forceful seizure of property. It is no use to pretend that none of these things happen. The course of liberation among the oppressed has included organized armed assaults on the structures of power.

Our native liberalism stops many of us dead in our tracks when we hear that violence seems to be a sanctioned way to solve problems. We not only believe ourselves to be a gentle people, who try to settle differences by peaceful means, but many consider ourselves to stand somewhere within the broad range of pacifist thought. We do not believe bloodshed solves anything. When liberation theologians, and the poor they represent, speak of revolution, they seem to mean more than friendly persuasion. If sticks and stones are all they throw at the police and government troops, it is often because sticks and stones are all they have. If they had guns and fire bombs there might be situations in which they would use them, or at least hold the coats of those who did.

At the 1983 Vancouver Assembly of the World Council of Churches, there was serious disagreement from the beginning as to whether the fundamental human agenda, and thus the agenda before the churches of the world, was justice or peace, meaning disarmament. The matter was never fully resolved. Those of us in the liberal churches of North America and Europe were convinced that first of all we had to pay attention to the threat of nuclear oblivion which hangs over the world, pushing the doomsday clock ever closer to midnight. On the other hand, those from the Third World claimed that disarmament was not their primary concern. They were not fascinated by the question as to whether the United States should put Cruise and Pershing missiles in Western Europe. Indeed they saw that issue as a sophisticated debate about ideology. The question asked by the oppressed was how and by what means they could get the boot of the oppressors off their necks so they could feed their children. Their concern seemed much more immediate and compelling to many of the delegates. The Assembly finally agreed that it was a both/and agenda, that there could never be justice without peace, but that neither could there ever be peace without justice.

In one sense, talking about peace is a luxury. People who are hungry don't have the time or the energy to discuss what it means that the United States has X billion tons of destructive power, and the USSR has Y. If you are hungry, without land, without recourse to the most elemental democratic rights, without standing in the courts, without the right of protest, without human dignity because you are viewed as a nonperson, what is the use of debating the relative merits of the Freeze resolution, or what ought to be in SALT III?

Your oppressors are not coming at you with weapons on the agenda of any forum concerned with disarmament. Of the 30,000 who have been gunned down by death squads in El Salvador in recent years, not one of them has been hit by an atomic device. They have been shot one at a time by simple hand guns and rifles, delivered not from intercontinental launchers, but from open trucks. What is the proper response to an oppressor who doesn't need nor would even know how to use tactical nuclear weapons? What is the use of talking about the elimination of the atomic threat when your children are ignorant because there are no schools in your village, sick because there are no doctors or hospitals, hungry because you have no land to grow food, and you stand powerless because what vote you might have is meaningless in a nation which will still be controlled by the oligarchy no matter who wins the election? What resource do people have when all the power is in the hands of the oppressors? Is violence ever justified?

Most ministers I know have a stack of sermons a foot thick deploring violence in all its forms as an appropriate response to evil. We want to be known as peaceful people. We know that the peacemakers are blessed. We read Jesus' injunction that if your enemy strikes you on one cheek you turn the other, that you love those who hate you, and that you put away the sword, because those who live by weapons will die by weapons. We cite the nonviolent power of Gandhi and Martin Luther King, Jr. We work for gun control legislation. When our government believes it can settle things by force or the threat of force, we exercise the democratic right of protest. We deplore the violence of capital punishment, even for the most brutal criminals: murderers, rapists, those who mutilate and destroy little children.

And then, with all of our pacific proclivities, we run up against liberation theology which fails to follow the path toward pacifism, and which does not speak in absolute terms about the use of deadly force. We read the word *revolution* which suggests that raw power is a legitimate way to solve the problems of the oppressed. If revolution means nonviolent, peaceful persuasion or a Gandhian satyagraha, we would be greatly relieved. But it often does not mean that, and anyone who has looked carefully at history knows it cannot mean that. The evidence seems to indicate that for the oppressed the way of nonviolence has rarely secured liberation.

Gandhi had the luxury of being up against a relatively civilized British society. Despite the excesses, colonial arrogance and even the occasional use of arms, there was not the wholesale butchery and dehumanization one finds among Latin American dictators. Gandhi's strategy worked in India, but would it work in Latin America? Liberationists seem doubtful.

Martin Luther King, Jr. was able to bring about a dramatic change in the lives of oppressed people in the United States by nonviolent means. But with all its shortcomings, the United States does respond to the persuasiveness of democratic pressures. King's movement was at least partly vindicated in acts of Congress and by a consensus of U.S. public opinion, which disavowed former patterns of discrimination and segregation.

Those who engage in the struggle for freedom in Latin America have no such comfortable social system against which to lodge their appeals. But the moment they move away from the gentility with which we are comfortable, or at least claim to be, they lose the support of many of our churches and their constituencies.

As a way to examine the issue of violence, I will suggest a perspective which may seem self-contradictory on its face, or at least situational, but I trust will provide a legitimate way to talk about this complex problem. The argument runs as follows. Under the ethics of the kingdom, violence used by the oppressors to ensure the domination of the oppressed is always unjustified, and outside the will of God. Violence employed in order to threaten, to control, to maintain power in the hands of the haves of the world is an illegitimate and unbiblical course of action.

The wretched of the earth, however, are faced with a different situation. Whether there is ever any justification for the use of violence by the oppressed is not a subject that we, who are the oppressors, can decide. We can make some proximate judgments, viewing the situation from our privileged position, but we cannot finally say whether violence is always to be condemned when employed by or on behalf of those who are the victims of repression, terror and intimidation. When viewed from the perspective of the oppressed, there may arise times and circumstances when all else has failed, and violence becomes a legitimate strategy.

Even if we allow the possibility of violence as an acceptable tool in the hands of the oppressed, it is always under enormous constraints. At the very least it may operate well within the guidelines of what has been historically called the just war theory. In considering the just war theory we must not jump to the conclusion that we have dusted off a handy excuse to be used by the rich and powerful nations vying with each other for hegemony over substantial chunks of the globe. We are only talking about people who have been crushed by institutionalized violence, and are seeking to survive.

In the pastoral letter on war and peace in a nuclear age, the U.S. Catholic Bishops outlined the constraints of the just war theory under the following categories:

1. It must be for a just cause: that is to protect innocent life, to preserve the conditions necessary for decent human existence and to secure basic rights.
2. The decision must be made by competent authority. In revolutionary situations there may be the "just revolution," which recognizes that an oppressive government has lost its right to claim legitimacy. (There was a document written in Philadelphia in 1776 which detailed the conditions which called for a violent response in what were then known as "The Colonies."
3. It must produce comparative justice. If violence means destruction and death, the result must be a more just society.
4. It must proceed from the right intention. Reconciliation, not victory, is the legitimate goal.
5. It must be a last resort.
6. It must have the probability of success. Under this rule, a just war must be a winnable war.
7. There must be a criteria of proportionality. No more violence than is necessary to secure the above-mentioned goals is allowable.

Even to contemplate the legitimacy of a just war thesis is

admittedly risky, fraught with loopholes, too easily usable to legitimatize violent solutions. Those who justify shooting at you today are not likely to love you tomorrow when the shooting is over; nor you them. History reflects few precedents for believing that revolution tends to leave in its wake a peaceful, let alone a just society. The exceptions have been when the oppressors are colonial powers who retreat to their own shores after the revolution. At least the founding of the United States followed those lines. The just war thesis is a way to help congregations discuss the issue—stand in the shoes of the oppressed—not as a readily acceptable solution.

Obviously anyone can claim to be "the oppressed." "We must stop the Soviet Union," we are told, "because their thirst for world domination can only be resisted by the threat of their own destruction." "What do you think should have been the posture of the U.S. church toward Hitler, who was exterminating entire populations?" "If your wife was being attacked by a gang of mad rapists, and the only way to save her life was to kill them, what would you do?" Those who are pacifists of one sort or another are often hit with such questions. Anyone who assumes simple answers to the complex problems these questions raise is naive in the extreme. I usually try to avoid responding to such baiting by insisting that I would have found a prior way to handle the situation without deadly force. I would try to make friends with my enemy before it got to that. I would argue even yet that there are always unilateral initiatives leading to bilateral disarmament; that these initiatives are both effective and consistent with the nature of the kingdom; that an intelligent response to evil, even by the oppressed, can and should avoid the use of force.

Yet putting the answers that way allows a certain luxury. I do not live in a village where if I speak up for freedom I can be taken to a country road and shot. I do not live in a place where my land has been seized to grow coffee for export when I need it to grow corn for my family. I do not have to face endless tomorrows at the merciless hands of oppressive powers, domestic and international, which control my destiny. For people in those situations to reject the use of violent methods may be to decide to stay in bondage. I who live in a land of plenty can sit comfortably and argue the merits of nonviolence. But my brothers and sisters in Nicaragua, El Salvador and South Africa do not have that luxury.

Enrique D. Dussel of Argentina, puts it this way:
> It is easy enough for people in the power centers of Europe, Russia and the United States to talk about nonviolence today, thereby disarming the struggle of the poor. But they have consistently violated and done violence to the poor of the earth. Now that their power grows more shaky, it is suddenly time to talk about nonviolence in the name of the gospel message. What hypocrisy from people who never defended the weak from the conquering arms of Europe and who now are trying to block the revolution of those on the periphery.[1]

As we have seen in the study of the Bible, God was not neutral. God stood with the oppressed, and often directed them to engage in liberating projects which were exceedingly bloody. The Exodus was not an act of gentle persuasion. Hugo Assmann, a Costa Rican theologian, finds in the New Testament a Christ who took sides.

> Christ's power is necessarily operative in a certain well-defined direction. It is on the side of the oppressed and against their oppressors. No longer is he the 'great reconciler' standing outside and above the conflicts that are going on here and now, although brotherly reconciliation between human beings in history is certainly the ultimate goal of his operative power. He is not a sectarian Christ who favors narrow partisanship and fanatically espouses a single tactic. But neither does he exercise his power apart from human history, operating in some isolated history of his own; his power takes sides in and through human beings.[2]

Assmann is correct; the Bible pictures Jesus, the Messiah, standing with the poor over against the powerful. While it is not widely argued that Jesus advocated physical violence, his "woes" directed against religious leaders of the day, his cleansing of the temple and his confrontation with both secular and religious authorities were aggressive enough to lead to his execution.

It must be noted, however, that even in the light of the possible justifications for violence detailed above, liberation theology has most often come short of an endorsement of bloodshed. In fact, beginning with Medellin and continuing until the most recent statements available, there has been a disavowal of violence on behalf of or by the oppressed. Segundo Galilea, of Colombia, describes how Christians must break the cycle of violence even if it means increased suffering.

> The pervasive violence on our continent is leading to political systems that are more and more repressive. They are both a cause and effect of the pervasive situation of violence. The vicious circle created by the various symptoms and forms of this situation constitutes the worst possible oppression of human beings. We must break that circle. Liberation from violence is one of the most important tasks confronting Christianity today. . . . Violence is a collective kind of sin, or a collective temptation if you prefer, and as such it must be redeemed at its very roots. Here we have an open door for the message of Christian liberation.[3]

Both in the documents and praxis of liberationists we find little evidence that violence has been seen as a legitimate alternative. The blood spilled has most often been their own. We cannot make claims for the universality of restraint, and it is quite likely that even within the basic communities there have been guerrilla activities and revolutionary cadres. But thus far, on the whole, the Christian stance has insisted on peaceful solutions.

While eschewing a theological posture which endorses acts of violence, nevertheless liberation theology seems comfortable with words such as: "revolution," "struggle," "throwing off the yoke of oppression." The relationship between that kind of inflammatory verbiage and the tactic of nonviolence is as yet unclear.

Long before Gutierrez and Medellin, there were isolated heroes, whose passion for the freedom of the people led them to revolutionary activities. The most notable was Camilo Torres, a Colombian priest who was killed as a guerrilla insurgent near El Carma in 1966. He had been reared in an aristocratic family, and had become a priest out of a profound sympathy for the poor.

After serving for some years as a teacher at the National University, he began to denounce the inhumane treatment of the poor by the government, and was increasingly outspoken about the role of the church, or lack of it. When he refused orders to be silent, he was removed from his post and reduced to lay status.

Although stripped of canonical authority, Torres still considered himself a priest, and continued to work for reform within the governmental system. He next tried to emulate the tactics of Martin Luther King, Jr. His efforts at civil disobedience and passive resistance were met with increased repression, and he became convinced that armed revolution was the only alternative left. When he set out to join the guerrillas he wrote:

> I have ceased to say mass in order to practice love for people in temporal, economic and social spheres. When the people have nothing against me, when they have carried the revolution, then I will return to offering mass, God willing. I think in that way I follow Christ's injunction . . . 'leave your gift on the altar and go first and be reconciled to your brothers.'[4]

Although Torres became an ideological hero and role model for others, the movement has not been marked by a massive resort to or even advocacy of bloodshed.

Consider another kind of violence, not the violence of the oppressed, but the violence of the oppressors, what has been termed *institutionalized violence*. Section 14 of the Medellin document on violence points out that in Latin America even the absence of bloodshed should not be interpreted as the absence of violence. The control exercised by those in power may give the impression of the maintenance of peace and order, but in truth it is nothing but the continuous and inevitable seeds of rebellion and war which are being sown.

Section 16 defines the violence which surrounds the poor, whose lives are a mockery to decency. Every necessity is denied entire communities. The people are blocked from participation in any decision concerning their own welfare or fate. To hold people in bondage is what Medellin calls institutionalized violence. While decrying the violence contemplated by the oppressed, the bishops warned the oppressors: "One should not abuse the patience of people that for years have borne a situation that would not be acceptable to one with any degree of awareness of human rights."

Despite the restraint, one wonders how long the line will hold if the conditions of the marginalized continue to deteriorate. One only has to observe what has happened elsewhere in the world where the Christian commitment has not been as strong. At this writing there is increasing evidence that in South Africa, where 80 percent of the population are held to be noncitizens, a storm is brewing, and unless there are dramatic reforms by the white government, more blood may flow in the streets. Nor should we ever allow the warning by Gutierrez to move far from our consciousness: "There can be no peace without justice."

The real question of violence in the world is not whether the poor in the hovels of the Guatamalan countryside have the right to secure land for food crops by force of arms. The question is not even whether provinces in el Salvador act legitimately when brigades are organized for the purpose of holding onto land and resources against the central government, the oligarchy and the military, all intent on taking them away. The real question of violence concerns two other matters: the institutionalized violence to which Medellin refers and the massive uncontrollable violence inherent in the manufacture and deployment of major weapons systems and military apparatus by the developed nations of the world.

Until those larger issues are resolved, focus on the hypothetical violence of the oppressed is an exercise in hypocrisy. If we are to speak of violence, let us discuss the actual violence of the oppressors, not the theoretical violence of the oppressed.

U.S. trust in, use of and commitment to violence is not a new issue. The Americas, north and south, were conquered by violent peoples. The conquest of Latin America was exactly that, a military occupation of a land which belonged to someone else. The history of the control of that territory has been, from the time the Spanish landed until today, the tale of repression secured by overwhelming physical force. Populations were either destroyed or enslaved. Property was seized at gunpoint. Civilizations were dismantled.

The situation in North America was little different. Colombus, and the Europeans who subsequently arrived here, did not discover America. What they did was drive from the land those who already lived here, finally herding them onto reservations, destroying their culture and seizing all they held sacred.

When I was in grammar school I learned what every child in the United States is taught: we never engaged in an aggressive war. That is an untrue statement, beginning with the war against the native Americans. When we wanted part of Mexico we seized it. When we wanted Cuba and Puerto Rico, we found ready excuses to appropriate those territories. Being a religious people we often manufactured Christian sanctions for our military adventures. Why, we have never really fought wars at all; only religious crusades against demonic forces. One example will suffice.

In 1898 President McKinley, and the U.S. industrial interests which controlled him, needed a coaling station somewhere in the Pacific. To that end a U.S. expeditionary force seized the island of Luzon, then under the domination of Spain. McKinley knew he had a problem. He did not want the United States to appear to be an aggressive colonial power, yet controlling that far off place was in the United States' vital self-interest.

To justify his position, President McKinley enlisted God and when God told him, in prayer, that he had done the proper thing, that settled it. The President's spiritual travail was later reported to a group of his Methodist brethren.

> The truth is, I didn't want the Philippines, and when they came to us they were a gift from the gods. I sought counsel from all sides, but I got little help. I walked the White House floor night after night, and I am not ashamed to tell you gentlemen, that I went down on my knees and prayed to Almighty God for light and guidance. We couldn't give them back to Spain or turn them over to France or Germany, and it was obvious that the pagan Filipinos could not govern themselves, so there was nothing left to do for us but to take them, uplift them, civilize and Christianize them, and by God's grace do the very best we could by them. And then I went to bed and slept soundly.

THE QUESTION OF VIOLENCE 113

In a $29 million deal later concluded with Spain, we also got Cuba, Puerto Rico and Guam, the last place having been conquered by the expeditionary force on its way to the Philippines. Thus we made the Western Hemisphere safe from what Congressman McDowell delicately labeled "those murderous, treacherous, bull-fighting hyenas." So much for our historic commitment to nonviolence.

These acts of colonialism were the prologue to today's forms of institutionalized violence, and stand in secular history as the glory of the oppressors and the humiliation of the oppressed. Any school child will tell you they are part of our proud patriotic heritage.

After we achieved our "Manifest Destiny," and controlled this continent from coast to coast, we developed strategies which eventuated in our economic hegemony over the rest of the hemisphere. The Monroe Doctrine has been supplanted by trade policies which ensure that Latin American nations remain economic if not political dependencies. It is not that we are any more aggressive or mean-spirited than others, only that it is the tendency of large, wealthy, powerful nations to become larger, wealthier and more powerful. And that inevitably implies military force—violence.

We have already discussed the violence inherent in certain kinds of development. Liberation theology has sharpened the problem for us. As one U.S. theologian put it:

> A hearing of Third World theology must state plainly that United States economic development is seen as an overriding factor in Third World oppression. It is the clear conviction of Third World theologians, especially those in Latin America . . . that the United States is using up the raw materials of the Third World, as well as its own, in unprecedented fashion. In addition, to expand this level of development is not to solve humanity's production problems, but rather to compound them, since we are failing to recognize the exhaustible capacity of "natural capital."[5]

The United States is not only committing acts of violence against the peoples of the Third World who are alive today, but also gutting any hope their children have of escaping the chains of oppression. This route is taken with the realization it will require military might to sustain the imbalance. The oppressors are supplied with arms and other essential commodities necessary to maintain their advantage. When the subjugated peoples have been able to disturb the system and take the smallest first steps to rid themselves of the yoke of bondage, we have resisted their efforts, labeled them Marxist and threatened military remedies.

This is evident in our past interaction with Cuba and Chile. The United States has provided both military and "civilian" aid to bolster sagging governments in El Salvador, just as in Vietnam before we sent young men to die. In a mighty act of bravery the tiny island of Grenada was conquered. Nicaragua is held hostage to the United States, never forgiven for ridding itself of the malevolent dictator, Somoza. Instead of supporting her efforts to establish some semblance of just democratic rule, attempts have been made to isolate and destroy her economy. Since she had nowhere else to turn, she turned to Cuba and the Soviet Union, thus securing our uncompromised enmity.

On the other hand, the United States has been patient with the racist South African government and armed despotic regimes in South Korea, Taiwan and until 1986, the Philippines. All of these examples of institutionalized violence are laid on our doorstep. Can a new understanding of God's activity in history liberate us from these acts of violence which stalk the world?

Simultaneously at home how to handle the economic problems generated by the "glut of food" our farmers produce in a world where hundreds of millions live on the edge of starvation, is a topic of national debate. The failure to see the relationship between those two problems is the kind of institutionalized violence which results in the deaths of tens of thousands every year. The artifical manipulation of the prices of crops and other raw goods, for the sake of transnational corporations is a form of violence. Unemployment and underemployment, which are deemed necessary to hold down interest rates and inflation is a form of violence. If we have no other answers than these, perhaps we need to examine our economic system.

The question we must confront as we are addressed by liberation theology is: How can we be set free from these sins and their consequences? How can we throw off the bondage with which we, the oppressors, have lived? Those are the theological issues with which we must struggle. It is within the struggle we will find our project, the way in which we engage in the liberating praxis which is the outbreaking of the kingdom in our midst.

We have all seen the statistics which detail how the people of the United States, who are but six percent of the world's population, consume 40 percent of the world's resources. The data is often accompanied by a model of the world reduced to a village of 100 people. More than 50 are destitute. Three or four are affluent—and so on.

During a sermon I once distributed slices of bread among the congregation, using that statistical data base. Some worshipers got two or three slices; some one; most a corner of a piece; many more of a crumb; and a few, the starving, received nothing at all. I then raised a number of questions: How did those who had little or nothing feel about those who had more than they could use? What would you do if you were in one of the latter categories, and became increasingly aware that while you were perpetually hungry there were those who had to "build bigger barns" to store what they couldn't consume? If God is a God of justice, the kind of God the Bible describes, with whom would God stand? Would God, and those with whom God had identified, take any direct action to remedy the imbalance? Is violence inherent in that kind of world, and if so, at whose doorstep does the violence lie?

If the answers to the questions are clear, where does that leave those who, in fact, have a huge chunk of the loaf? We clearly are the ones who are inflicting violence and death on the world. What action do we take once we hear the gospel, once we become committed to the same kind of liberation we believe God is committed to?

We cannot complete our review of violence without examining the second issue raised at the beginning of this chapter: the massive violence of the U.S. weapons systems, and the military apparatus which surrounds them—the actual physical violence or threat of violence, which has become national policy. Not only is the inequity in goods and services heavily weighted in the United States' favor, but we are gutting the economy, as well as the world's supply of nonrenewable resources, to ensure that the balance remains where it now is. In the middle years of the 80s, the United States is spending in excess of a third of a trillion dollars each year on what is called *defense*. Defense was not always the proper word. When I was growing up that arm of government was called what it had been called since the founding of the nation: "The War Department." In an attempt to discard the assumption that war was inherent in national policy, some years ago the name was changed to "The Department of Defense." I had always believed the change to be no more than a literary slight of hand. It was still the war department!

The truth is, the change in name was an accurate recasting of the reality. Most of these enormous sums will not be used to conduct war. In fact, as things now stand, very little of it will be used to shoot at anybody. It will be used exactly as the title implies, in defense. And what is it we will be defending? We will spend ourselves into economic oblivion to defend the existing distribution of the world's goods. We will defend our right to pay farmers millions of dollars of non-defense money not to grow food, in a hungry world. It is our way of life which is being defended. Now ask the question again: Where does the God of the Bible, the God of liberation and justice stand? With whom does God side in that kind of world? And what does the obvious answer to this question mean for us?

St. Paul called those things over which we had no control, but which shaped our lives, "principalities and powers." The final chapter of this book is about Christian hope, and the defeat of the principalities and powers, but other ground must be covered before approaching any profound word of hope. First we must deal with our compelling obsession to defend what we have with weapons we no longer control, from which we cannot hide, which we cannot lay down and which we cannot use; not one, not ever, not any place. That series of catastrophic dilemmas defines our captivity. It is not oppression in the same sense that the peoples of the Third World are oppressed. Yet we are not free to live fully human lives. We are not free to love our enemies. We are not free to create the kind of world where "they shall sit every man [one] under his vine and under his [her] fig tree, and none shall make them afraid" (Micah 4:4).

Our captivity is double. First we are burdened by all our goods. We pay terrible amounts of money simply to store them. Second, we have been forced to defend what we have with weapons over which we no longer have control. We are in the iron, or should we now say, the nuclear grip of the principalities and powers.

Several years ago I spent time among the monastic communities of Mt. Athos in Greece. There are no roads, only treacherous mountain footpaths. It requires both will and endurance to make one's way from one monastery to another. There is a sea route, but even that is fraught with difficulty and danger. When I arrived at the port of entry of this independent state, I decided to set out over the mountains for the monastery of Stavranikita, several miles distant. It was a blazing hot day. I carried, in a large suitcase, all the things North Americans "need" for such an undertaking. I had packed several changes of clothes, cameras, toilet articles, extra shoes, a cassette recorder, books and paper, an alarm clock and ten pounds of assorted junk I never traveled without.

By the time I reached the foot of the hill from which can be seen the stark outlines of the monastery, I was observed by a monk, whose possessions could have all been put in a small plastic bag. He had taken note of my plight and had greeted it with gales of laughter. I was so weary I was barely able to walk. I made out a few words through the avalanche of merriment with which I had provided him. "Baggage, baggage, look at the silly American with all that baggage! Why don't you throw it in the sea? You are weighed down with all your impediments." What I carried were my impediments! I was not free as he was free. If I wanted to be free I must dispose of all those things which weighed me down. I must throw them into the sea!

I was reminded of Jesus' words about those who drag their impediments around with them, who spend their lives worrying and fretting about things. "Consider the lilies of the field," he said. I had not learned then, nor have I fully learned yet, that freedom may consist in taking Jesus' advice, and that of the laughing monk. I could not throw into the sea what I carried, which meant I was doomed to be weighed down, immobilized, chained to what I owned.

Consider how much more difficult would have been my plight if I had been forced to carry two pistols, an M-16, a grenade launcher, a swarm of B-1s, eight Trident submarines, a couple dozen *peacekeepers* and all the other paraphernalia—impediments—it would have taken to defend what we, the affluent, lug over the mountains of the world?

We have already had a foretaste of what can happen if just a tiny bit of the violence we carry around with us is ever used. A few years back I visited a high school in the downtown area of a major city. Like every other building in the city, it was new. An old man, who had been principal of the school years ago, told how he was away on business the morning 320 students and 12 teachers were killed. The school stands about two miles from ground zero in Hiroshima.

In the early 80s a nun was brutally murdered in Amarillo, Texas. The city was in an uproar, crying out for vengeance. Amarillo is where the bombs are assembled. In Hiroshima, on August 6, 1945, three entire orders of nuns were liquidated. Each modern bomber, aloft and on missions today—missions from which they have thus far always turned back—carries a single bomb with the explosive power of 500 weapons the size of the one which leveled Hiroshima.

What can you do about it? What can your congregation do? What can the entire Christian enterprise do? We have no power, it seems. We are captives, oppressed by taskmasters over whom we have no control. We are caught in a web spun by cosmic forces, the principalities and powers.

Perhaps we can never really understand the oppression of the poor. We are not poor, nor are we likely to become so. Their experience is not our experience. A theology of liberation which speaks to them does not speak to us in the same way. But perhaps we can begin to identify with their plight when we come to terms with the depths of our captivity to the principalities and powers. To be oppressed is to have no answer to a system which enslaves, demands obedience and from which we cannot escape. If that is the case, we are part of a creation still in chains, a creation which the coming of the kingdom will set free. For now we cry out: "Who can deliver us from this body of death?"

Having felt the whip and chains of our captivity, we may be ready to listen. First there will be the voices of the Third World's oppressed, as those voices come to us through the theologians who speak together with them and on their behalf. But behind their words we must begin to hear the voice of God, and listen for God's footsteps in our history, coming to our aid, championing our cause, engaging in acts of liberation on our behalf. Our task is to discover the project which announces, declares and portends God's kingdom, and gives evidence to the will of God being done on earth as it is in heaven.

Notes

1. Enrique D. Dussel, *Frontiers of Theology in Latin America*, ed. by Rossino Gibellini. SCM Press, 1980, p. 205.
2. Hugo Assman, *Frontiers*. p. 145.
3. Segundo Galilea, *Frontiers*. p. 175.
4. Jorge Lara-Braud, "What Is Liberation Theology?" 1981. (An outline of lectures, Westminster College, Cambridge, England).
5. McElveney, *Good News*. p. 11.

8

The Oppressed Too Close to See

Most of the sources used in this guide for congregations are from Latin American or Third World theologians. Every writer must define the boundaries of a study or nobody would ever complete a book! There are obviously significant numbers of persons not in the Third World who are also oppressed, or who speak for and with them.

The oppressed too close to see are difficult to categorize. They are first of all the poor, the homeless, the hungry who live in the midst of the affluence of the First World. They are our neglected and malnourished children. They are the elderly, who live on marginal incomes and less than marginal hopes. The oppressed too close to see are often to be found among racial minorities (a different situation than in the Third World where the oppressed are often majorities).

While the plight of women might lead us to see them as a separate group, in reality most of the poor are women and their children, and perhaps the most neglected, women and children from racial and ethnic minorities.

This chapter will suggest some introductory questions they raise for the life and work of our congregations.

Consider first the plight of the poor in our communities. If liberation theology is rooted in liberating praxis, that is changing the world not just describing it, we are at a disadvantage if we confine our concern only to distant peoples with whom we have little direct involvement. Praxis may indeed begin among those in our midst, who are not free because they are caught in the oppressive structures which have simultaneously provided us "the good life." The immediate temptation is for church folk to play Lady Bountiful, delivering Thanksgiving baskets to the poor. That kind of maternalism has long been a way to avoid dealing with the basic structural issues which undergird the institutionalized oppression already discussed.

Even though as an interim strategy we may "give a fish," or even "teach to fish," the major task still lies in removing the fence between the oppressed and the river. It may not even be our task to dismantle the fence, but only to identify with the oppressed, and celebrate the ways in which they take down the barrier. The shock comes when we realize the fence has protected our right to monopolize the river bank! Without the liberating power of the Holy Spirit is it ever possible for people to choose, voluntarily, alternatives which violate their own economic self-interest? I am not aware of examples in which an affluent oligarchy has said: "Because it is the just and honorable thing to do, we will change the laws which have provided us much more power and wealth than anyone else." The Constitutional amendment giving the U.S. Congress the right to tax the incomes of its citizens, and their corporations, may be the one exception.

Over the long haul, more is entailed than passively watching what the oppressed do, although that is how we learn our first lessons. Pope John Paul II verbalized his active identification with the poor when he said to a group of marginalized Central American Indians:

> [I am] your voice, the voice of those who cannot speak, or who have been silenced. [The pope] wishes to be the conscience of consciences, an invitation to action, to make up for lost time. We must act promptly and thoroughly. . . . We must implement bold and thoroughly innovative transformation. Without further delay, we must undertake the urgently required reforms. . . . It is not just, it is not human, it is not Christian to continue certain situations that are clearly unjust. [We] must implement real, effective measures on the local, national and international levels.[1]

Insofar as the Pope called for action, not just reflection or discussion, he was affirming what liberation theologians had been telling him for some years. The traditional theological models have often been so caught up in rational discourse and scientific inquiry that they have not seen that the acts of liberation always define the starting point. Elizabeth Schussler Fiorenza, a feminist theologian who understands the priority of praxis, puts it clearly when she insists:

> [The] specific issue of contention between so-called academic theology and all forms of liberation theology . . . is the insight that all theology knowingly or not is by definition always engaged for or against the oppressed. Intellectual neutrality is not possible in a historical world of exploitation and oppression. If this is the case then theology cannot talk about human existence in general, or biblical theology in particular, without identifying whose human existence is meant and about whose God biblical symbols and texts speak.[2]

James Cone, a black liberationist, defines academic theology in what approaches absolutist language:

> *A rational study of the being of God in the world in light of the existential situation of an oppressed community, relating the forces of liberation to the essence of the gospel, which is Jesus Christ.* This means that its sole reason for existence is to put into ordered speech the meaning of God's activity in the world, so that the community of the oppressed will recognize that their inner thrust for liberation is not only *consistent* with the gospel, but *is* the gospel of Jesus Christ.[3]

If Cone seems to be overstating the case, or limiting theology so that it has no meaning apart from a particular relationship to the plight of the oppressed, nevertheless he moves theology from speculative twittering to liberating praxis. Cone's words are not far from those of Martin Luther: "Not reading and speculation, but living, dying and being condemned make a real theologian."

To a significant degree we in mainline churches have distanced ourselves from active involvement with the structural or institutionalized oppression which marginalizes persons in our own communities. We have said too little and done less to alter those sturdy cultural fences which keep the poor in our midst from the river. We have done fairly well in acts of charity resulting in a two-tiered class system, which is one of the reasons why we see so few of the poor sitting in our pews. We have also encouraged the government to modify its social programs so that some persons are taught to fish. When national administrations have threatened, or actually dismantled programs for the marginalized and needy among us, we have raised our voices and engaged in modest amounts of political badgering. But we have not often challenged the fundamental structures which predetermine that there will be no employment for too many, the control of wealth by too few and the perpetuation of systems which demean workers and make them expendable pawns in games played for very high stakes.

What has been the posture of our congregations, for instance, when there has been a strike, or a serious effort by labor to share more adequately in the "American dream"? What have we tended to do when a corporation decides to close a large factory in spite of the fact the closing will result in hardship, unemployment, suffering and dislocation among the workers? If government support is provided the corporations, through tax breaks and subsidies, but no consideration given the labor force which had depended on the factory, how do we morally justify that position? Can a society be called *just* when the only factor to be considered is *profitability*? What about the people who have been abandoned in the cities of the Northeast and Midwest by capital's headlong flight to the sunbelt?

Occasionally middle class churches move beyond the level of charity. At the 1985 General Assembly of the United Reformed Church of the United Kingdom, the question was raised as to what the denomination might do if it suddenly found itself in possession of a considerable sum of money earmarked for the relief of the poor. The speaker, who was presenting a report from the church's division which handles social ministries, insisted that to take the funds and divide them among poor people would be inappropriate. A better alternative, she suggested, would be to use the windfall in lobbying the government to alter its policies. At the time the government was busy cutting back on "welfare state" programs. The suggestion was well received by the Assembly, even if the delegates knew the point to be moot. It was like telling a friend what we would do if we suddenly discovered a rich uncle had died leaving us ten million dollars.

If the speaker and the assembly were on the right track, they were still far short of the destination liberationists would have suggested. In the first place, no middle-class religious institution is without major funds or the power to generate them. Both better stewardship and a radical reordering of priorities would produce the money, once it was decided the funds had to be obtained. In the second place, the suggested solution still leaves the power, the wealth and the decisions in the hands of those who have had that trinity of authority all along. "We know what is best for you, our poor children," is an attitude we will leave behind, once we hear what liberation theology is all about. We have not heard what the poor of the world are telling us as long as we insist that we know what they ought to have.

In a restructured social order the advice givers and the advice takers are not differentiated. A just society provides ways in which each social group is responsible for making decisions about its survival. What voice do the workers have in a decision to close or relocate a plant? When every judgment is based on how it affects the "bottom line," those who own the means of production are the only ones whose opinions and lives matter. Justice, however, demands that everyone affected by the results of a decision ought to share in the decision. If, as Reinhold Niebuhr said, "Justice is the only legal tender of love in the world," then justice is acted out good news—the gospel. The insistence on justice is, therefore, evangelism.

Many magnificent examples exist in which the church has stood not just for, but with the oppressed. During the 1984-85 miners' strike in Great Britian, many congregations in hard hit areas became focal points for organization and action, at a time when large numbers of working class people had dismissed the church as useless.

Consider the testimony of a pastor in South Wales. Over the

course of the strike he got to know the leaders of the workers, as well as the colliery managers who were his usual constituency. He traveled to London with labor officials in an effort to identify with the desperate situation of the strikers. He grieved with them when: "hopes of justice and reconciliation were dashed by what seemed to be a handful of men—and a woman—who lived light years away from the struggles, hopes and fears of the South Wales miners." Even though the strike was not settled, it was decided that the only thing to do was for the miners to return to work. The Rev. John Morgans tells the story of the day the pits opened after a year of violence and misery.

> We decided, as a family, that we would walk with the miners as they returned to work. At half-past six we joined the procession as it wound its way up the barren valley to the pit, ushered by church bells and led by the Tylorstown Band and the advancing dawn. A remarkable moment occurred as the 600 miners stopped to line the road and applaud us, their friends; and then for us, the supporters, to clap in these friends, not one of whom had broken ranks with their comrades. At least now there was a renewed sense of dignity of being a miner.[4]

In this account the church did not take over or assume leadership. The struggle was in the hands of the oppressed, not the middle class. The task of the church was to stand with, to become one with, to be in the midst of. That is often a difficult role to play. We are used to having not only the honored seats in the synagogue, but the head tables during discussions of the problems of the poor. To stand down, listen and support the structural changes the oppressed opt for is often a painful business. What they decide may not always be in our interest. If the poor get bread, we may not get as much cake. They may not put the issues in the polite way we want them put. They may not always want to play by the gentlemanly procedures middle-class people admire. But as Cone says:

> When the oppressed affirm their freedom by refusing to behave according to the masters' rules, they not

only liberate themselves from oppression, but they also liberate the oppressors from an enslavement to their illusions.[5]

What and where are the pockets of oppression in your community? Who are the marginalized? What ways can your congregation support them as they find an effective voice in the decisions which concern them? Are there members of your congregation who need to be evangelized so they can discover the relationship between their Christian commitment and decisions they make beyond the walls of the church? What political changes would have to take place in your community for "justice to roll down like water, and righteousness like an everflowing stream" (Amos 5:24)?

Consider now the racism which still haunts our society. There is no need here to review the sordid history of slavery, segregation and bigotry, nor to describe the church's complicity almost every step of the way. If apartheid in South Carolina and apartheid in South Africa are divided by an ocean and a generation, nevertheless they are, or were, of the same order. According to Pastor Babundha Kabongo-Mbaya of Zaire, the oppression of the black people of the world cannot be seen apart from colonial history, a major part of which concerns the introduction of slavery into the western hemisphere. He cites a request in 1870 by missionary bishops in Africa who asked the Pope to release the black race from the curse of Ham!

For many Africans, liberation implies regaining the integrity of their own traditions, religions and mores. While many westerners quake at an amalgam of what they term "tribal superstitions" with the Christian faith: "the African theologian wants to give Christ a black face without disfiguring it."[6]

A First World response to the situation in Africa must take the form of political action. At this writing the continued involvement of the U.S. government and U.S. business enterprises in South Africa, without demanding that the 80 percent black majority in that land be treated as persons with basic human rights, is a disgrace and a scandal. Desmond Tutu, Anglican Archbishop of South Africa and winner of the 1984 Nobel Peace

Prize, put it this way:

> In the long term, the solution must be political. There are no two ways about it. Either there is going to be power sharing or there is not. If not, then we must give up hope of a peaceful settlement in South Africa. . . . Blacks will be free whatever you [the South African government] do or don't do. . . . Don't delay our freedom, which is your freedom as well, for freedom is indivisible.[7]

Even following the "victories" of the civil rights movement, the problems in the developed world are only different in degree, not in kind, from the problems in South Africa. Despite all that has been done in the past generation, Sunday at 11 A.M. is still the most segregated hour of the week. Even so, as we have known for many years, the problem goes far beyond integration. A knee jerk reaction which does nothing more than fit minorities neatly into an alien majority culture is not to read the gospel from the point of view of the oppressed, let alone act on that reading. Some hold that integration is, in fact, a hindrance to liberation.

James Cone is the best known black liberation theologian in the United States. His message is only secondarily directed to the white community. We can learn, however, by overhearing it:

> . . . He [Jesus] is our contemporary, proclaiming release to the captives and rebelling against all who silently accept the structures of injustice. If he is not in the ghetto, if he is not where men are living at the brink of existence, but is, rather, in the easy life of the suburbs, then the Gospel is a lie. The opposite, however, is the case. Christianity is not alien to Black Power; it is Black Power.[8]

The middle-class church will have only the illusion of freedom until the racial minorities within our midst are free under terms which they have defined. Every community has the official version of "race relations" and the unoffical version. Hyde Park, the home of the University of Chicago, is the best, most peacefully integrated neighborhood to be found in any major city. That was the official version. One only got the unofficial—true—version by talking to the black young people on the streets. What is the unofficial version in your community, and how is the church addressing the issues it raises?

Special attention must be given to the plight of women, particularly poor and marginalized women in our society. "Women's liberation" is not a fad. Insofar as it calls for justice in a social milieu where illustrations of injustice can and do fill volumes, it is akin to Third World liberation movements. At one end of the scale there are increasing numbers of middle-class women who are no longer content to be pushed to the sidelines and who are properly demanding elemental justice. But of even greater concern for our study are the desperately poor women and their children, who believe they are without power or control over their lives. As Elizabeth Schussler Fiorenza puts it:

> If liberation theologians make the "option of the oppressed" the key to their theological endeavors, then they must become conscious of the fact that "the oppressed" are women.[9]

Fiorenza also asserts that historical theology must include the interpretation of the biblical records from a feminist perspective, something academic theology has been hesitant to accept. How long it will be before we can learn to think about theology and the biblical witness from a feminist perspective remains to be seen. It is a subject, however, with which every congregation must struggle.

At this writing the fundamental issues of justice for women are only beginning to come into the awareness of most churches. Until a decade ago the congregation I serve, which has attempted to take the themes of liberation seriously, had no women involved in the liturgy except on Women's Sunday, nor women on the governing bodies and certainly no woman could have been considered eligible to be the presiding officer. As in many of our churches, that day is happily over. Women's Sunday is a thing of the past, and women serve equally throughout the life of the congregation. Our struggles, however, have just begun. We do not yet know what to do about language, particularly in hymns and in the biblical record.

Outside the parochial boundaries, while we are sympathetic to the problem of injustice in the marketplace, we have yet to develop the appropriate strategies by which we stand with the oppressed, as they seek to remove the fences between themselves and the river. Women are paid substantially less than are men for the same work, or work which requires similar skills or effort. We are currently graduating substantial numbers of women from our seminaries. We believe in equality, at least that is our stated position. When it comes to welcoming these same women to ecclesiastical positions, there seems to be some distance between our articulated positions and our actual practices. What about your congregation?

Notes

1. Boff, *Salvation*. pp. 233-4.
2. Elizabeth Schussler Fiorenza, *Challenge*. p. 93.
3. James Cone, *A Theology of Black Liberation*. Lippincott, 1970, p. 17.
4. John Morgans, "Report to the General Assembly of the United Reformed Church of the United Kingdom," 1985.
5. Cone, *A Theology*, pp. 185-6.
6. Babundha Kabongo-Mbaya, "Minutes of the European Conference of Churches," 1976.
7. Tutu, *Hope*. pp. 101-2.
8. James Cone, *Black Theology and Black Power*, p. 4.
9. Fiorenza, *Challenge*. p. 92.

9

Congregational Praxis

We now turn more specifically to the work of the congregation. The thrust of this book is to assist congregations in finding ways to examine their captivities, and thereby claim the freedom which is the gift of Christ. But no book which deals with liberation theology can be limited to an examination of issues. We are not describing an ideology, we are encouraging liberating praxis!

This is not a handbook, a how-to-do-it compendium of programs useful in making your congregation a "liberation church." I doubt if such a book could be written. We are not talking about a promotional scheme or next year's mission emphasis. Nor are we providing a list of techniques.

Liberation theology is finally a theology; or to be more specific, it is theology, an action-oriented, thoughtful encounter with the God of history. We experience the activity of God in three ways: the creation, the incarnation and the persistence of grace in our history and in our midst. That encounter comes not in words about events, but in the events themselves. The Trinity is not a doctrine. It is rather a symbolic system given to the three ways God acts "for us and our salvation."

Even though liberationism begins with action, many congregations face a frustrating obstacle. Most of us are rational people. At least that is how we want to be viewed. Indeed we do tend to proceed deductively. We define the problem, gather premises, evaluate them, draw hypotheses, test them, review the results, test them again and finally agree on the nature of truth and its theoretical application to "real life situations." Liberation theology proceeds from quite a different perspective—how to change the world—not just understand it. This more inductive way to think is difficult for many, and it is doubtful if we shall have much influence on people by assuming that they can think in any other way than they are used to thinking.

In some arenas we already know it is easier to act our way into a new set of feelings—or beliefs—than to think our way into a new set of actions. At times we simply act differently and discover that what we believe has been modified enroute. Many counselors come upon situations in which helping people change their actions is far more helpful than getting them to change their minds.

What is true in personal psychodynamics is also true in social and structural relationships. During the civil rights debates we were often told: "You can't legislate morality. You can't get people to accept integration by passing a law." History has proved them wrong. To the extent that the U.S. South today has modified the practice of segregation, attitudes have also been changed. Neither set of changes came about because masses of people suddenly thought differently about racial issues. Laws were passed mandating a change in actions. Attitudes were modified because behavior was first legislated. Legislation does not tell you how you must feel, or even what you must think, only how you shall or shall not act.

Effective action is not willy-nilly irrational flailing. There must be, simultaneously, the rational work necessary to make the argument. Enough members of Congress first had to be convinced that Jim Crow laws were contrary to the spirit and meaning of the "American dream," or they had to believe it was in their political interest to say so. Martin Luther King, Jr., and others in the civil rights movement, basically religious people, acted from clearly articulated presuppositions, most of which were worked out enroute. They knew they were headed to "the promised land," but the map was drawn while they were on the trail. It was their action/reflection style which prepared the ground for the political decisions which followed.

In chapter two, we described how many of the base communities in Latin America were formed. You recall the initial thrust was Bible study. Action did not develop out of thin air, but out of a confrontation with the biblical account of God's activities in the midst of an oppressive situation. If action is prior to doctrine, it is first of all the action of God, whose works have wrought our salvation. We know God by what God has done, not by what God has thought. The biblical record is a recital of the mighty acts of God.

The two activities, study and action, cannot be seen as separate endeavors, one following the other, but as simultaneous activities. It is not that we study the biblical record so that our actions might be changed. After all, many people in our congregations have been pouring over these texts for decades without it seriously affecting the way they act. Nor is the study of liberation theology simply a prologue preparing us to do something about the world's oppressed. If to know God is to do justice, knowing and doing are two sides of a coin on which heads and tails appear simultaneously no matter which side is up. Study and action in a congregation move together, parts of a single theological system.

Many of the things a congregation can do may not even be seen, nor do they need to be, in the context of liberation theology. We all know church members who would immediately be turned off if they thought what they were doing was related to what was going on in Latin America. On the other hand, where possible it is important that congregations discover what liberation theology is and what its effects have been in the Third World.

We are on dangerous grounds when we try to argue with political conservatives, who are probably also religious conservatives, on secular theoretical grounds. Our argument must be theologically and biblically based. If Christians do not draw their social ethics from the Bible, then where in heaven's name do they get them? "You have been a member of this congregation for thirty years. You rarely miss a Sunday. You have taught a Bible class for two decades. Tell me, as a biblically literate Christian, how you justify your political position." I have found variations on that question a compelling way to do evangelism among the half-washed who fill the pews of our churches.

Many churchmen and women have not heard the gospel because it has not been spoken, let alone acted out, in their midst. What they have gotten from the pulpits are lectures about personal morality; explanations concerning the nature of God; advice on how to be successful and happy; the affirmation the United States is great because the United States is good. Biblical teaching and preaching, beginning with the overlay which sees God as liberator from sin and its consequences, may help satisfy the spiritual starvation rife among religious people of the First World.

To learn about and understand liberation thought is to look at both the Bible and the world through the eyes of the poor. Liberationism was not discovered two decades ago by a Peruvian priest. It dates from the earliest records of the Judeo-Christian tradition, and is well within orthodox Christian faith.

If those in our congregations have ears to hear, and the gospel is proclaimed, they will be confronted with what God is doing in the world. From there it is not far to the celebration of the victories of Christ, evidenced in the liberation of the oppressed. When people inquire as to what God is about, they can be told what Jesus had the disciples of John tell their jailed leader: "the blind receive their sight and the lame walk, lepers are cleansed and the deaf hear, and the dead are raised up, and the poor have good news preached to them" (Matthew 11:5). Better yet, they can be shown outcroppings of the Messianic age in their own communities as well as in the Third World.

Before dashing off onto the green fields of congregational action, we had best pause for a moment. Frantic undifferentiated activity for its own sake may be the sign of irrational agitation, not evidence of the Messianic age. We must again remind ourselves that it is not the church's task to bring in the kingdom. The notion that the fullness of the kingdom will be revealed in the creation of a perfectly just society is always the risky vision toward which liberation moves. Those theologians who tend to come closer to the Marxist analysis often appear to identify a classless society with God's kingdom. Those who see the fatal shortcomings of Marxism, and are not caught up in notions of the perfectibility of society, hold that the kingdom in all its fullness is the sign of God's final triumph, not the product of human initiative or work.

Only a cursory look around will provide abundant evidence that human ingenuity, work and fervor have not and will not "bring in the day of brotherhood and end the night of wrong." Godlessness and inhumanity seem never to end. Even after 2000 years of Christian history, half of the world's population lives on the edge of despair. Liberation theologians take that analysis seriously. But they do not hold that the church is, therefore, relegated to a passivity which only awaits the last days when God will finally establish the kingdom. While awaiting God's reign to dawn, an intermediate step is mandated. The church has been commissioned to produce signs of the kingdom—outbreakings, evidences, a foretaste. The church becomes God's beachhead in this troubled, sinful world. The church is given a project, not to bring in the kindgom, that is, to perfect society, but to give evidences of its coming.

As we engage with God in the task assigned us there is actually a change in the social fabric. We discover a reality as well as an anticipated fulfillment. God is already at work in Christ, who has ushered in the Messianic age, which is itself the penultimate step on the way to the kingdom. The church is called to continue the work begun in the incarnation. It is to declare the liberating actuality of the Messianic Year of Jubilee. In stating this was "the acceptable year of the Lord," during his appearance at the synagogue in Nazareth (Luke 4:16ff), Jesus linked Isaiah 61:2 with Leviticus 25 and Deuteronomy 15. These latter texts established the ground rules for the Year of Jubilee and the freeing of slaves.

Evidence from the Dead Sea Scrolls supports the notion that contemporaries of Jesus were making similar linkages. There is no indication, however, that the Jubilee had been observed in Israel's later history. If the Year of Jubilee had until that time been little more than a divine rubric, it was now, in the work of Christ, an actuality!

If Jesus' announcement affirmed that something new was occurring in human history, as did his mighty works which were seen as outcroppings of the Messianic age, it follows that the church is under orders. It is commissioned to witness to the new age which had been inaugurated in the coming of Jesus. The church is to be the foretaste of life in the kingdom. It is a demonstration project, a beachhead in hostile territory. Its works are to be the works of Christ, and even greater works, through the power of the Holy Spirit.

What does it then mean for the church to assume the project Christ gave it when he commissioned it to proclaim the good news—the liberation of the oppressed—to all the world? As we have seen throughout this book, what it means for the basic communities of the Third World and what it means for middle class congregations of the First World may be quite different. Each part of the church seizes the specific project Christ has assigned it. Each seeks liberation from the specific captivities in which it and its people are caught. Each also celebrates what God is doing for the other. Specifically then, what are the implications for congregations? We will first deal with our project in relation to the oppressed, both in the Third World and those too close to see. We will then look at the captivities which arise out of our peculiar social context.

The way we receive the new life in Christ, and by which that life is continually refreshed, begins in God's act. God's salvation has already been secured for us in the death of Christ. By baptism we have become inheritors of all the promises of God. Yet we continue to live under the curse of sin and its consequences. This was Paul's lament, and it is ours. It was painful for him, as it is for us, to realize he continued to miss the mark. What he did, he detested; and what he should have done, he neglected. He knew that he could only be made whole by the mercy of Christ. But until he realized his sinfulness he could not even make that affirmation.

In one sense, to become aware of our continual sinfulness is a matter of education. We learn the ways in which we have denied the grace of baptism. It is a shocking discovery for the individual Christian, or for the church, to realize that in the account of the Exodus we are the Egyptians. It is a discovery we will resist with all our strength. We will look for back doors, find ways around, produce excuses, deny the reality and do whatever else is at hand to extricate ourselves from the accusation that we, by the way we live and who we are, have caused our brothers and sisters to make bricks without straw.

I know of no easy or painless way to face our sinfulness. It is not only that the oppressed of the world are marginalized, but that they have been marginalized so we might live "the good life." What is even more shocking is, if God has taken sides with the oppressed and is acting to free them from their captivity, we cannot escape the plagues!

Every preacher wishes there were a comfortable way to put it. If we could only find the right illustration, the softer words, the appropriate stories by which we could avoid or even cushion the hard truth, we would be relieved. But the gospel confronts us just as Nathan confronted David, "You are the man!" From that judgment there is no escape, no easy way out. The only way out is not to put it out at all, which is what happens in many congregations in the First World.

The first step lies, therefore, with our preachers and teachers. No congregation likes a steady diet of bad news. Indeed, the gospel is good news, and preaching which is a weekly twenty minutes of eye gouging is rarely redemptive, either for the preacher or the congregation. After just so much of it, people quit listening. Proclamation which is not heard is not edifying.

Without hedging about the imperative of the witness, or dodging a single issue, I am now convinced that the appropriate way to begin is not from the pulpit but from the teacher's lectern. Every congregation has within it persons who hunger for biblical literacy, who want to understand what the Latin Americans are talking about and who are hounded with the gnawing sense they are not free; despite their affluence. They are also vaguely aware that the plight of the world is laid at our doorstep. They believe the Bible may have something to say about these matters, although they have never figured out just what. Nor have they been provided the tools to understand the biblical account or to see the relationship between liberation theology and what they have been called to be and do. Teaching can begin with this ready group.

Two extended courses of study come immediately to mind. The first and most obvious is Bible study, with the overlay described in chapter five. In our congregation I take twenty students at a time, and lead them through an introduction to the Scriptures. It takes two years of hard work to complete the course, one year in each Testament. Visitors are not encouraged to attend, and once the group is formed new students are not enrolled. Each student is expected to do the necessary class preparation. No one comes and sits. Notes are taken, assignments done and regular on-time attendance required. Those who miss a class are asked to review the recording made of the lecture and discussion. Students who complete the course not only have a reasonable grasp of the biblical materials, but have seen them through the eyes of the liberating work of God. The drop-out rate after the two years is about 33 percent.

The second course of study is a simple invitation to learn about liberation theology. It is hoped that this book may provide a basic resource for such a course.

For some time within my denomination, I have been pleading for the recovery of Bible teaching with the children of our congregations. When a people forgets its stories, can no longer tell the children the meaning of the testimonies and the statutes and the ordinances which the Lord God has commanded, that society is in serious trouble. Theological and biblical illiteracy among adults is the fruit of a second generation of our failure to provide youngsters with the basic biblical accounts, and then to help them understand what the stories mean.

Someone should write a systematic biblically oriented curriculum for the young from the perspective of the liberating activities of God. I don't think I have ever met a child who wasn't ready to hear a story. I suggest that our teaching techniques in the church school, no matter how it is organized or what it is called, revert to storytelling with a hermeneutic which sees God's liberating work in history and is geared to the age of the child. Even without a professionally prepared curriculum, children can learn what it means that "we were Pharaoh's slaves in Egypt; and the Lord brought us out of Egypt with a mighty hand."

In addition to Bible stories, there can be developed or there may already be written, parallel accounts about the experiences of children in the Third World. Given the biblical base suggested above, children can understand liberation theology. I am not talking about introducing them to the writings of Gutierrez or

Boff. I'm not even sure most adults in our parishes are equipped to handle that kind of data. But children can understand stories about Jose and Maria, what happened in their village and in their families and how they got a school and a hospital and a little piece of land to grow beans.

Another educational resource is to be found in the use of firsthand witnesses. Few communities are more than an hour's drive from Christians who have recently been to Latin America and have seen what is happening in the churches there. Scores of clergy and layfolk carry a literacy about liberation theology from firsthand observation. In addition, there are refugees, exiles and permanent residents who have come here and can speak about their own lives.

All of these suggestions fall under the umbrella of the teaching ministry of the congregation. Most congregations only need to expand somewhat their notion of what their educational program can and should involve. While it is true that information in itself doesn't produce action, among the base communities Bible study often generates praxis. They, however, tend to see a direct relationship between their economic, political and social situation and the biblical message. We tend to see the Bible as interesting information. Although liberation theologians insist that action takes place and then reflection, in our experience no one goes until they are sent, and no one is sent until they hear the word.

If teaching is the primary way to address the issue in the typical middle-class congregation, preaching must follow close behind. This volume does not have the room to offer a detailed analysis of preaching on liberation themes. I suggest the same approach recommended in the previous section on teaching. Storytelling has reemerged as a fundamental homiletic art form. Of course one begins by telling Bible stories. Many of us follow a lectionary as the basis for choosing sermon texts, and the question is raised as to whether that tends to be restrictive. It is my experience that neither preaching on liberation theology, nor on any other theme, is best done by using pet texts. The lectionary saves the preacher from riding a few horses to death.

When, however, one uses the overlay, or hermeneutic, suggested in chapter five, the Bible is discovered to be a rich source of the evidences of God's liberating activity in human history. When we allow the Bible to tell its own story we never need to force a liberation theme on the text. The theme will arise naturally out of the text.

As is also true in teaching, the best way to interpret what is happening in Latin America, or other places in the Third World, is to tell stories. These stories become sermonic windows, illustrations of the essential biblical message. The material available is almost without limit. The simple recitation of events has power in itself. History used as story is far more compelling than grinding away at ideology or complex doctrinal notions. Often the preacher will not even need to make the point. The story itself makes the point. We have all heard good stories ruined by preachers who tell them, and then go on to point out what we ought to do in light of the story, or what the story really means. Letting the story act as its own vehicle is a powerful way to present what you want to say. At times, Jesus interpreted one of his stories, but most often the story had to stand on its own merits. Going on to make the point would have taken the edge off the story and Jesus was too good a Rabbinic craftsman to do that.

Many sections of the Bible obviously articulate liberation themes. The Psalms are songs of liberation. The prophetic writings tell stories of how God challenged the royal consciousness with an alternative consciousness, as Walter Brueggemann has so powerfully pointed out in his book, *The Prophetic Imagination*.[1]

Other parts of the Bible, which seem less likely to offer a biblical base for liberation themes, also contain rich and powerful stories of God's liberating work. When one is made aware of the underlying context of the particular book or historic era, the theme comes clear. It is not that we see the mouse because that is all we are looking for, like the pussy cat who went to London to visit the queen, but that what has been there all the time naturally emerges once we are confronted by the God of history, who always stood by the oppressed and marginalized. Although we do not usually see it in this light, because we have not used the liberation overlay, even the book of Revelation is the announcement of God's victory over the principalities and powers, all dressed up in apocalypic language. Reread the letters to the seven churches found in the first three chapters, and you will discover they retell the story of the Exodus in different language and with an eschatological emphasis.

To illustrate how liberation themes are found to be at the heart of the most unlikely circumstances, let us examine one of the least likely of all, a situation in which God seems to stand by the oppressors and not the oppressed. I refer to the conquest of Canaan by the tribes of Israel. I have often wondered how that would read from the perspective of the Canaanities! Here they are living peacefully, and up from the south comes this thundering band intent on conquest, booty and a radical displacement of the Canaanitic culture. If the liberation theme holds, and God stands on the side of the oppressed, then why aren't the Canaanites, those being marginalized, and the invaders only an ancient version of the Spanish conquistadores? One might wonder whether the post-Exodus stories of Joshua and Judges are nothing more than a strained apology for a bloody invasion under the banner of just another tribal war god.

Read these stories again. They are about the liberation of the oppressed! In his monumental work, *The Tribes of Jahweh*, Norman Gottwald argues that the Jews, between 1250 and 1050 BCE, were not the bloody conquerors usually pictured, but rather a small group of liberationists who had come out of Egypt and were joined by the marginalized people of the area in battles against the rich and powerful, who ruled the city-states of Canaan. The wars of conquest were fought to establish a more equitable society for the masses who populated that part of the world at the time this small band of freedom fighters arrived. Gottwald's book runs over 800 tightly packed pages, but consider one brief quotation. Gottwald puts the following question in the mouth of the Canaanites: "What is it we notice in Israel that makes these people different?" The response, for which he argues at length, goes as follows:

> We notice that Israel is a total community that confronts and challenges us to join in its way of living. To do this we have to relinquish voluntarily or involuntarily the old forms of sociopolitical domination,

> including the old religious ideologies. Israel calls us to a new form of social relations which destroys class privileges. For those of us enjoying class privileges there is nothing but the prospect of loss as Israel grows stronger. For those of us who have been exploited by the privileged classes there is the uncertain promise of a better life in the Israelite alternative. Others of us, neither at the top nor at the bottom of the social order, enjoying both advantages and frustrations as agents of the class rule, are torn in our responses to Israel. All of us in the old feudal social order respond to Israel and her religion in terms of perceived threat or promise to our whole existence in society.[2]

Gottwald insists that the Canaanites would not have noticed that Israel had an unusual belief in a particular God, and a distinctive set of cultic practices by which that God was worshiped. It was not a matter of taking on another religion, but rather a call to a whole new liberated and liberating style of life. What we have in Joshua and Judges is a revolution instigated by a tiny determined band of outsiders, who won the allegiance of the marginalized living in the midst of and beyond the walls of feudal city-states ruled by despotic kings.

Judges were raised up by God when Israel forgot the mandates of justice and equity, and reverted to the worship inherent in the old despotic systems. The calamity finally came, at least was conceived, when Israel decided she ought to have a king, like all the other nations. Samuel resisted that move for reasons which he clearly articulated.

> These will be the ways of the king who will reign over you: he will take your sons and appoint them to his chariots and to be his horsemen, and to run before his chariots; and he will appoint for himself commanders of thousands and commanders of fifties, and some to plow his ground and to reap his harvest, and to make his implements of war and the equipment of his chariots. He will take your daughters to be perfumers and cooks and bakers. He will take the best of your fields

and vineyards and olive orchards and give them to his servants. He will take the tenth of your grain and of your vineyards and give it to his officers and to his servants. He will take your menservants and maidservants, and the best of your cattle and your asses, and put them to his work. He will take a tenth of your flocks, and you shall be his slaves. And in that day you will cry out because of your king, whom you have chosen for yourselves; but the Lord will not answer you in that day (1 Samuel 8:10-18).

But they wanted a king, and a king is what they got. If you read the rest of the story you know what happened. By the time Solomon came along, Israel looked like and acted like the very nations and petty kingdoms the earlier movement had sought to overcome; only much more powerful and repressive. The revolution fell into the same trap as the system against which it had previously revolted. Such seems to be the lamentable history of revolutions. The exploited northerners finally would have no more of it, and at the death of Solomon executed their plot to be rid of the bondage into which they had fallen. It did not take long before the north was sucked back into the old trap, this time under the cover of Baalism. By the time the eighth century prophets came on the scene in Samaria and Bethel, the needy were sold "for a pair of shoes" (Amos 2:6).

This account, which is but one narrow slice of the biblical record, illustrates that preachers are not reduced to the five or six pivotal texts usually cited by commentators on liberationism: the Exodus, Jesus' appearance in the synagogue in Nazareth, the parable of the last judgment, etc. The whole of the Bible is available. The use of a lectionary becomes a disciplined way to discover how profoundly liberation is rooted in biblical history. From the story of Noah until the final triumphant themes in Revelation, the Bible is the declaration and record of God's liberating activity. I don't know how liberation theology can be avoided once one is aware of the river of freedom coursing through both the Old and the New Testaments.

Having talked about teaching and preaching, we must move to action of a more public sort. The question arises: How does a congregation in the First World participate in the ongoing liberating activity of God in the Third World? What does congregational praxis mean once we have heard about the oppressed and marginalized, and seen ourselves as the oppressors? This is a difficult question. In the long run liberation comes as God works with the oppressed, not with the oppressors. There is little evidence in the biblical record that God had much success with the Egyptians. In fact, the resistance to the freedom God was to bring was so deeply rooted in the royal consciousness, the text describes how following each plague "Pharoah hardened his hearts and did not let the people go" (Exodus 8:32). Oppressors do not often see the light and unlock the prisons without being coerced.

The liberation of the oppressed is not ours to produce. Our role may only lie in ceasing to be oppressors, for our oppressiveness is our captivity. As we begin to understand what holds us in bondage, and how we are captives because we are involved in an unfree system, we may identify with our oppressed brothers and sisters. Both they and we may realize all of us are subject to a wickedness greater than any of us.

Consider an image which comes from the liberation of Jericho recorded in Joshua 2 ff. Gottwald argues that God was intent on freeing the city, not just for the sake of those who came up from Egypt, but in order to establish a more just social system for the residents of Jericho itself. To that end the assistance of a harlot, who lived in the city's wall, was enlisted. Rahab obviously knew about the siege which was to take place and, being part of an outcast social group, identified with the impending revolution. While sharing, albeit marginally, in the old order, she became an advocate for the new order. She realized that the liberating work was in the hands of others. There was not much she could do, but what she could do she did.

The analogy cannot be pushed too far, but there may be some clues here for us. Assume we are cast in the role of the harlot. Even though we have made our living in the midst of the oppressive society, we recognize that we, too, suffer a loss of freedom simply by our identification with that society. Because we come to believe it is God's purpose that freedom be a universal actuality, not only are we hungry to be set free, but we are in solidarity with those whose oppression is far worse than our own. In fact, we see in their liberation ours as well. If they are freed, then we are freed, both from our role as oppressors and from those chains which are peculiar to our own captivities.

Two specific courses of action may occur to us:

1. To modify the situation within the wall; that is to exert pressure on the political structures—an option probably not open to Rahab, but available to us.

2. To assist the forces of liberation operating outside the city gates in whatever way we can.

We have previously discussed whether or not the church should be involved in the political arena. We assume the appropriateness of that endeavor. The question is: How shall the congregation make an effective witness? The simplistic answer is self-evident: in whatever ways citizens of the nation in which the church is located do it. If that is the obvious answer, it is not always the available one. The caveats we cited which arise out of the constitutional mandate concerning the separation of church and state are enforced through the tax codes. Religious institutions are prohibited from significant engagement in political action, although that phrase has not been tightly defined. The church, of course, is perfectly free to violate those laws if it is willing to give up its tax free status.

The current trade-off may not be worth the price. Although the laws were written to protect freedom of religion, we may be coming to a time when the church realizes it runs the risk of being bought off. The price of its silence is very high. If efforts are made to further limit the role of the church in commenting on and engaging in matters of public policy, we can expect to see religious bodies reexamine their favored institutional status. A few within the church now maintain that it should pay its way, and thus ensure its independence, whether or not the law is changed.

On occasion the church, fully aware of the consequences, acts outside the law. These situations arise when there is need either to demonstrate that a particular law is wrong or as an appeal to a moral authority higher than any civil code. The literature about civil disobedience, and its consequences, is voluminous.

At times the church consciously violates the law in order to save lives. One current issues may serve to illustrate how this matrix of law, conscience and liberation often produce a complex ethical dilemma. Shall or shall not congregations provide sanctuary for those the government says are illegal aliens? The legal ramifications concern congregations which had decided to shelter refugees, particularly from Guatamala and El Salvador. Abundant evidence exists which shows that if many of these aliens were forced to return to their home countries, they would face prison or even death. The U.S. government does not consider them political refugees. Since the U.S. government supports the regimes of both nations, it would obviously be embarrassing to harbor political refugees from friendly nations. Those who have escaped the terrors of Marxist governments are warmly welcomed, while those who come from equally tyrannical right wing regimes are not.

Given this situation, congregations across the land are doing what the government will not do and declares illegal for churches to do. They have welcomed these refugees and have provided a safe place for them. At this writing the response of the government has been tentative. At no time have the police or the immigration officials entered a church, or interfered with the housing and entertainment of these "illegals." Providing transportation, particularly from city to city, has marked the vulnerable crack. Arrests have been made on public highways, and prosecution initiated. A recent case in Arizona resulted in the conviction of Christians who provided sanctuary. The government maintains that acts of sanctuary are violations of the immigration statutes, but seem hesitant to enforce them. Churches which have openly declared themselves sanctuaries have taken a major step in identifying with the oppressed in act as well as word.

While this book is not a compendium of what congregations might do, I believe the commitment to act will itself produce possible courses of action. Once Christians decide to act, God will provide the avenue for that action. In the town where I live, groups from several congregations and ecumenical agencies agreed to take seriously the task of raising the visibility of the conditions of the marginalized in Latin America. Besides meetings, projects, seminars and workshops we were able to sponsor "Four Days of Freedom," a Fourth of July celebration in our community which addressed a larger set of issues. In addition to a celebration of our nation's liberty, the focus was on freedom for the oppressed in Latin America. Films were shown. We had brown bag discussions. And, the observance was climaxed by a noon rally on the steps of City Hall, commemorating our independence and the struggle for freedom by people far removed. For the better part of a week at least one community faced the repressive conditions in Latin America and the complicity of the U.S. government, a point of view which otherwise would not have been articulated, at least to that wide an audience.

Most mainline denominations and judicatories, and a few congregations, believe large concerns can be addressed by passing resolutions. Many issues involving the plight of the oppressed in the Third World are, however, far more complex than resolution writers realize. Instead of adding to the dialogue and contributing to the consensus, our statements are often an embarrassment. If the church chooses to take positions, often a fruitful tactic for raising the consciousness of religious constituencies, it ought to be intelligently done. I do not want to discourage the generation of positions papers by our congregations, judicatories and assemblies; only that it be done as wisely as possible. Many of our churches have untapped resources. We have economists, business people and a host of qualified technicians who do understand the issues, and who ought to be enlisted in any effort to affect complex matters. Too often these persons are left out of the discussion, or it is assumed ahead of time they not take a helpful position. We must tap these resources.

Another increasingly popular form of witness has been for an individual or a church body to purchase shares and attend stockholders' meetings of corporations known for their repressive policies. Unless massive amounts of data are first collected and assimilated, the effort will look foolish and ill informed. With the proper homework, it can be a powerful tool.

While it has limitations, due to the short duration of most visits, sending members of the church—well prepared—to the Third World has been an avenue through which many congregations and communities have developed a better understanding of what is really happening. Most urban congregations include business persons, who in the course of their work move within the Third World. Groups of churches can hold regular briefing sessions for them, so that when they go they will be more immediately aware of the conditions of the oppressed and the political, economic and social matrix of which the oppressive situation is the result.

Other avenues for action also exist in most alert church bodies. Letter writing, confronting your member of Congress when he or she is in the district, trips to Washington, D.C., the "Action Network," Riverside Church's Disarmament Program, demonstrations, picketing, denominational peace and justice action groups are but a few. Only the limitation of our imaginations blocks us from seeing or creating opportunities to stand with the oppressed and engage in the necessary political work it takes to alter policies which make us the oppressors.

We now turn to ways in which liberation theology provides the occasion to confront the captivities afflicting individuals, which arise out of our particular cultural circumstances. If in Christ we are to be set free, evangelism, and here I speak of the conversion of persons, must be the way persons are introduced to the fullness of the liberating gospel. Conversion must be understood, however, not as joining our institution, taking on a new set of doctrines or getting a first-class ticket to heaven. It must be dramatic transformation of life, which leads to the liberty freely offered the children of God. Conversion is not a response to a membership recruitment drive. It is a radical response to the gospel. We do not down-play the need for personal conversion, even if we have previously argued that evangelism has much broader perimenters than that. The conversion of persons is not an option for the congregation. As Emilo Castro, General Secretary of the World Council of Churches, has put it:

> To proclaim the kingdom is always an invitation to join the forces of the kingdom and to enter into the kingdom. Repentance is the first act of response. Sins are confessed, allegiances changed and attitudes transformed. . . . the word conversion has been misused; it has been reduced to mean a psychological experience. We need to recover the meaning of the word for the

act of response to the call of the Servant King, Jesus Christ, that will send us, as the Father sent Jesus, sustained by the Spirit, along the same path of suffering and hope.³

In addition to preaching, which we have discussed, the liturgical life of a congregation can be dedicated to the proclamation and celebration of the liberating life God has offered. Prayer is at the heart of, not alien to, liberation thought. Can any pastoral prayer, or the intercessions of the church, fail to include those in the congregation who are captives, as well as the marginalized of the world? I think not.

Worship is a celebration of the mighty acts of God. It is the joyous announcement that Christ has set us free from all those things which have held us in bondage. The liturgy not only announces the liberation of Christ, but it is also a call to participation in the project of God's kingdom. Central to our liturgical life is the celebration of the Eucharist. In addition to its memorializing emphasis, it is a foretaste of the feast of the kingdom where all oppression and captivities are gone. It is the sacrament of the kingdom. It is an anticipation as well as a commemoration. It announces the Lord's death, "until he comes" (1 Corinthians 11:26). The Eucharist is not an individual act, not my quiet time to be alone with Jesus. It is a feast of joy in which we join with the whole company of saints in heaven and on earth to declare God's ultimate victory over sin and death.

Throughout the work and ministry of the congregation, as well as in its liturgical life, we need to be aware of the importance of the words we use. I refer specifically to the use of inclusive language. The first time I encountered it I was taken back, but the more I heard the benediction which includes the words; "the Lord make his face to shine upon us and be gracious to us; the Lord lift up *her* countenance upon us and give us peace," the more appropriate it sounded. I would encourage the use, or the adaptation, of the inclusive language lectionaries produced by the National Council of Churches.

Fewer resources are more troublesome than the hymnal. Many otherwise solid hymns are no longer usable. As beautiful as it is in sentiment and poetry, I doubt if we can anymore sing "O brother man, hold to thy heart thy brother." Some hymns can be redrafted, although one needs to exercise great care. Using inclusive language is one small way in which congregations can take seriously the problems of the marginalized too close to see.

Emilo Castro insists that rites, such as the baptism of little children and weddings, ought to be occasions for the celebration of the liberating message of the gospel.

> The baptism of a child reminds the family and the community that the child is called to be a co-worker with God in the shaping of creation, and the building of community. The celebration of a wedding . . . is a commissioning of the couple to contribute to the life of the whole community. . . . Every activity of the church should thus be seen in terms of its calling to proclaim the kingdom.[4]

Perhaps the most helpful conceptual framework in which to capture the broad range of liberation motifs in a congregation is "shalom." It is a much more profound word than peace, although it includes that concept. It refers to a fullness of life, a plenitude, richness, roundness of human experience. It more often refers to social groups than to individuals. A society living under the power of shalom has beaten swords into plowshares and spears into pruning hooks. Shalom defines the society in which everyone "sits under his vine and her fig tree, and none shall make them afraid" (Micah 4:4). Shalom of God is explosive. There can be no shalom for one until there is shalom for all.

In my denomination certain churches have agreed to be called "shalom congregations." The designation suggests the direction in which a congregation wills itself to be moving, not a destination at which it has already arrived. Not only is world peace part of the self-conscious mission of shalom congregations, but they also seek avenues by which the church witnesses to the kinds of peace which set us free from the principalities and powers, the demons and destructive forces which ensnarl and oppress persons.

One other liberating movement has episodic currency—the small group movement. In the Third World it has taken the form of basic communities we have already discussed. In the First World it may take a number of quite divergent forms. In some congregations, members are divided into groups of about ten families called "house churches." Each of these groups has a specific set of functions. They are more than ways to "keep track of the membership." Nor are they reduced to providing a handy tool for conducting the annual financial campaign. They can be serious study groups. One congregation used house groups to study the World Council of Churches document, "Baptism, Eucharist and Ministry." Another congregation encourages small groups of people to meet and look not only at the stewardship of their members in terms of what they give to the church, but how they use the rest of their incomes. Still other small groups have certain goods in common. Why should ten families each buy a lawn mower when one could do the job for ten neighborhood homes? The money which might have otherwise been spent is allocated to some ministry important to the group.

The small group holds significant possibilities for congregational praxis, and may indeed help shape the religious style of the future. Yet in our culture such endeavors seem to dissipate rather quickly, and those who are committed to them often end up more isolated and oppressed than they were at the beginning. The house church or small group, used as an instrument of liberation, probably works best when it is held accountable by the larger congregational structure. Our captivities do not usually occur in small groups, but in broader social movements. To be free from oppression must be more than increasing the size of our prison cells.

Leslie Newbigin suggests that we ought always be on the lookout for new liberating structures.

> When the whole of society . . . is baptized and the Church is the spiritual arm of the establishment, the critical role of the Church devolves upon separate bodies—the monks, the radical sectarian groups, the million and one movements on the fringes of the Church.[5]

Karl Rahner states: "The church of the future will be built from below by basic communities as a result of free initiative and association."[6]

It is quite possible that the current structures are so rigid, cracked and unrepairable that God will raise up new ones; new wine skins for a new day. The clue may be in the formation of the basic communities among the poor. The era of denominations and even congregations, as now known, may be coming to an end. Yet while we welcome new structures and celebrate the gifts God gives us through them, we should not yet abandon congregations as the basic avenue for the proclamation of the gospel. In our culture they are yet the best way to proclaim release to the captives, to engage in liberating praxis, to declare that the kingdom of God is at hand.

Notes

1. Walter Brueggemann, *The Prophetic Imagination*, Fortress Press, 1979.
2. Norman Gottwald, *The Tribes of Jahweh*, Orbis, 1979, p. 596.
3. Castro, *Sent.* p. 76.
4. *Ibid.*, p. 91.
5. Leslie Newbigin, *Your Kingdom Come*, The Preachers Press, 1980, p. 28.
6. Karl Rahner, *The Shape of the Church to Come*, SPCK, 1974, p. 108.

10

The Liberating Power of Passion

Having come thus far it might seem that liberation theology is pervaded with a certain gravity, a heaviness or grimness. Indeed it is a serious business. There is little joy in the grinding despair of the marginalized or in contemplating that we must share responsibility for their plight. Even certain of the key words we have used have a square jaw character.

Praxis does not immediately send a spark of zestful energy coursing through the body. It has an artless sound about it. Indeed, as the word is used in Marxism it tends to cycle down into bureaucracy, and bureaucratic systems tend to be monochromatic. Traveling in Marxist nations one is often struck by a singleness of color. Everything seems battleship gray, from the mood of the people to the color of the buildings.

The word "project," which we have used throughout this guide to signify the role the church is called to play, also strikes us as being a ponderous technical word. If Marxism has led to a monochrome world, western technology with its project orientation has led to a pragmatic efficient one. Feelings, either of joy or grief, have little room in a well run technocracy.

In the days when divers were let down into the depths of the sea in insulated suits on which heavy metal helmets were mounted, there was always the risk that an accident would sever the diver from the air supply above; or some malfunction in the equipment controlling the rate of descent would plummet him downward until he would be crushed by the enormous pressure

THE LIBERATING POWER OF PASSION

of the water. If he descended far enough, the pressure on the body would be so great that when pulled to the surface, the entire corpse, or what was left of it, would be found to have been squeezed into the helmet. One wonders if the middle-class religious enterprise has not attempted to squeeze the whole body of Christ into the helmet of rationality.

I am concerned that the church, at least the church as we middle-class, mainline, First World people experience it, tends to be devoid of passion. Why is it we seek so few working class people in our worship services or in other phases of our parish programs? Why is there such a sense of loneliness and boredom pervading our congregations and our extra congregational religious institutions? Why do so many of us find it necessary to live safe, prophylactic, adventureless lives?

Liberation theology offers a way out of the grimness of our spiritual ennui and our prophylactic lifestyles. The path from boredom to freedom runs through the highland of passion. If we are to be set free from our captivity to the grayness, which marks the religious climate of our congregations, it will be as we recover the bundle of emotions, feelings and energies called *passion*. The freedom and adventure passion brings may enable us to discover the robust life, the full life Christ promised those willing to take the risk of faith.

I am well aware of the problems inherent in emotional religion. Emotion runs along a narrow ledge and is always in danger of falling into the valley of fanaticism, and religious fanaticism trades in the demonic. The fanaticism of fundamentalists, be they Protestant fundamentalists in the United States, Moslem fundamentalists in Iran, the Lutheran fundamentalists who confronted the peasants in Germany, or counter-reformation fundamentalists in 17th century Spain, is always bad news for people who live in the neighborhood.

Emotionalism also easily leads to sectarianism, and sectarianism easily leads to intolerance, persecution and pogroms. Hitler insisted on a religion which carried the German people ahead on wave after wave of heartfelt devotion. "Ein Volk, Ein Reich, Ein Glaube," he shouted at them, "One people! one nation! one faith!" "The Christian faith will safeguard the souls of the German people," he roared.

Although the danger of being overcome by the irrational emotionalism which leads to fanaticism and sectarianism exists, I doubt if that is our problem. Our prison bars have been forged by the ennui mined from the rock-strewn arid ground of rationalism. Our prophylactic prisons are emotional ice castles become jail cells.

In marriage counseling perhaps the most common lament heard is "The passion has gone out of our relationship." There are, of course, the fresh hormonal waves of physical passion among the newly married or the young. But there is also the mature, vital, life-giving passion that must thrive in any marriage if it is to remain generative. I have known people married sixty years whose relationship was still passionate. They fought, they loved, they argued, they laughed. The fire was always there. I have also listened to couples who could not love because they were so polite to each other they felt nothing. Any human relationship without passion is already headed toward the graveyard. So is a passionless religion. A recovery of passion is one key to our liberation.

From beginning to end the Bible is a passionate book. In the creation narrative, when God had put the finishing touches on the project, God said to whomever was listening, "That's very good" (Genesis 1:31). It was with pleasure God created the heavens and the earth. The drama of the Exodus, the archetypal event for liberation theology, is an emotion packed story. The song of Moses, sung by all the people of Israel (Exodus 15), is a feeling charged cry of victory. When David brought the ark to Jerusalem it was accompanied on its journey with "shouting and the sound of the horn." The king himself was "leaping amd dancing before the Lord." Some people always look down their noses at such emotional displays and Michal, David's wife, was so put out with her husband's religious excess she read him the riot act when he got home. "I will make merry before the Lord!" David countered. But the passion had gone out of the marriage and the text adroitly says: "And Michal had no child until the day of her death" (2 Samuel 6:16-23).

The Messianic story describes profound levels of feeling. "God so loved the world . . ." is hardly a statement subject to a rational interpretation. "Faith, hope and love" are feelings, not just ideological modes of piety. We call the story of the suffering and death of Christ, "the passion." How can one read the account of the suffering servant in Isaiah as the intellectualized statement of a religious system? "He was despised and rejected. . . . He has borne our griefs and carried our sorrows . . . He was wounded for our transgressions, bruised for our iniquities." In Gethsemane his sweat was like drops of blood. He wept over Jerusalem and outside the tomb of his friend Lazarus.

Commenting on the events of Jesus' last week in Jerusalem, Jurgen Moltmann says:

> One does not understand this passion history if one sees in it only one more tragic incident in the long history of humanity's suffering. One understands the history of Christ's suffering only when one grasps the passionate devotion of Christ which led him into it and allowed him to bear it. And in the passion of Christ I see the passion of God himself and discover again the passion of my own heart.[1]

The appellation used more than any other in the gospels to describe Jesus' emotional state is "compassion." The word implies a passion which embodies the suffering of others; which takes it as our own. He had compassion on the multitudes—he felt the pain. It became his pain. Passion is not a Victorian philanthropic pity. It is hurting because someone else hurts. Christ's life of compassion ended in his own passion. He embodied, incorporated our sins and our suffering, our alienation and our oppression. "And with his stripes we are healed." That is compassion!

Could it be that only by our passion, only by feeling the suffering of the oppressed, only by taking their alienation as our own can we be brought to life? Is their suffering our salvation? With their stripes are we healed? Could compassion be the remedy for our ennui? Could we too be perfected because we suffer along with the suffering? Is compassion the way to escape the prophylactic life?

Anger is another passion. The cleansing of the temple was a passionate act. The woes against the religious leaders were passion ridden blasts. The muteness at his trial was the fury of silence. Why the anger? How did it also shape his compassionate passion? It was an expression of his intolerance for the injustice of his day. His friends were the marginalized. He loved them passionately. They were the left out, "the spat upon and ratted on." The sick, the lepers, the Samaritans, the neglected and forgotten and despised—he had the wrong friends for a religious man, so claimed his enemies. He was always off the mark when he talked about issues which concerned the least advantaged of his day. And he got upset when the religious leaders could not see what was happening to the poor, the afflicted and the excluded. They had little compassion, and they could not deal with his. But Jesus could not lay his anger aside, even for the sake of social harmony. His virulent compassion led to his passion. He was unable to accept what he knew to be unacceptable.

Consider the fog-shrouded middle-class church and its members. No dancing before the Lord, not in our congregations; and little compassion which turns to passion. Pity, yes; works of charity, yes; but not blazing anger, which declares that we cannot accept the unacceptable circumstances in which the oppressed and the marginalized live. Not much and not often. So we respond with a "tut, tut" in a world which calls for a compassionate-passion laden response.

If the terms *praxis* and *project* strike us as prosaic, the images of the Messianic age throb with feeling. Freedom, liberation, opening the prison doors, releasing the captives, are hardly gray terms. Jesus' promise of liberation—that we should have life and have it fully—overflows with dynamism. The robust life he promised is hardly a static or reflective condition. If we have not sensed it perhaps it is only that we have yet to hear the gospel. Again the answer is evangelism. Liberation theology is committed to radical change, which means conversion. It is not getting society understood which is at issue, but getting society reordered. It is not talking about what it might mean to be free from our captivities, but breaking open our prisons which is the goal.

How do we, in our middle-class congregations, capture that dynamic, that life-giving energy? The answer is clear: live as those who are being set free. That is an action orientation, not an ideological or reflective one. It is possible for us to act our way into a new set of ideas more quickly than we can think our way into a new set of actions. A perennial question in both Britain and the United States is how we combine evangelical enthusiasm with theological integrity and appropriate action. Left to its own, the rich emotional life of many evangelicals turns on itself, like the horns of a cow, which twist back as they grow, finally penetrating the brain. Choosing between that and the emotional sterility of the more traditional church is a dismal decision. Liberation theology may provide the bridge, a third way, a formula which combines theological integrity, emotional depth and an authentic understanding of mission.

I return to a concern about the liturgical life of our churches. The Sunday morning service is still the heart of congregational action. I doubt if the question for most of us is how to develop new styles of worship. Some parishes can incorporate fresh liturgical forms with grace and authenticity. But how do we take the traditional liturgy and use it to celebrate our liberation? For many, worship has become a dull rational exercise, a sign of oppression, not freedom. Perhaps we do not need to create a joyful, Spirit-filled worship service, only to act as if that is what already is.

> Moltmann says:
> Is not the experience of the presence of God the most joyful thing in the world? Is not Christian worship the feast of the resurrection? Why then are not our worship services liberating feasts of heaven and earth, of the body and the spirit, of the individual and the community?[2]

Moltmann suggests that modern enlightened Protestants have reduced the liturgy to doctrinal and moral instruction. He believes we have much to learn from the free worship of the African church, as well as other Third World Christian bodies not limited by the Enlightenment. Although many of us would gag at the notion of drums and dancing, let alone hand-clapping and foot-tapping, I believe much of the solution revolves around getting our bodies back into the liturgy. Worshiping God from the neck up denies the incarnation; that is, it denies we are bodies, and that the body is designed for God's glory.

Many of us in the United States' most middle-class institution, the liberal Protestant church, have all but eliminated the use of the body in worship. We drape our clergy in dull black robes as if they had no bodies. We neither kneel nor raise our hands in prayer. We use candles only as decoration. We would be horrified if we were assaulted by the odor of incense, and scandalized by the ringing of the bells at the moment of the consecration of the bread and the wine. And as for bread and wine, we tend to use bird pellets or paper thin wafers, and non-wine.

Our hymns are sung more ponderously with every passing decade, or so it seems. Hymns were written to be joyful expressions of the raging rivers of religious sentiment—music and poetry are arts, not sciences—but we denature them by dragging them slowly down a dry creek bed. If we are making a joyful noise to the Lord one would never know it by looking at the faces of most of the worshipers, who appear to be suffering from some slight intestinal discomfort. And where is there an opportunity for members of the congregation, unless it is officially listed on the program, to say what is on their hearts, to ask for the prayers and support of the congregation, to thank God for a healing, or a victory, or a joy or a liberating mercy?

Jesus did not talk about the kingdom in terms of solemn services. He talked about wedding feasts. In what sense does the usual "celebration" of the Eucharist resemble a wedding feast? Not only are the hymn tunes even more dirge like, they are probably the most introspective, somber, melancholy poems in the book. What if we sang Easter hymns at communion? What if we took the same liturgical patterns familiar to us and infused them with a new sense of liberating joy? If they began to feel like the feast of the kingdom, might not they become so?

Again, we are not only talking about positive or affirmative feelings. Many of the most profound feelings we experience are bitter, negative, heart wrenching. If we tend to be embarrassed about expressions of joy, how much more do we shy from overt expressions of grief. What would happen if someone in your congregation got up in the middle of the service—or even at a time designated for that kind of concern—and said, "I hurt! My daughter has been picked up in Denver on a drug charge. I don't know what to do!"

I have seen that happen, and the reaction is not what one might expect. All over the congregation people moved from their seats until this woman was surrounded and held and affirmed. If there were those present who would use the event as an occasion for gossip, the church needs to deal at a later time with their particular captivities. Nobody gave her an answer. There were no easy answers. But the church provided her a way to shake off the captivity of immobility and isolation which had kept her from doing anything, except suffering.

What does all this have to do with liberation theology? Everything! If we are not oppressed economically, we are oppressed by the loneliness and ennui which grip middle-class society. As we study the Bible through the eyes of our own oppressions, we are encountered by the God who stands with the lonely, the left out and the distressed.

In the part of the world where I live we do not even allow death to be a time for the church to share in the grief and mourning of the bereaved, to weep with those who weep. Funeral homes, which appropriately care for the physical remains of our dead, see it as their primary business to care for the grief stricken as well. This function belongs to the church. I admit to almost a perfect record of failure in trying to convince even my progressive congregation of the inappropriateness of this division. In my ten years and over 300 funerals, there have been only six held in my church. The reasons are common: "That's not the way we have always done it in this community." "It puts a strain on the funeral directors. Holding the service at their establishment is much more convenient." "It didn't occur to me, and they assumed the funeral would be at the chapel." "If George is buried from the church I'll see his casket every time I come into that sanctuary, and I won't ever be able to worship there again."

It is the last reason which concerns me most. A spiritualistic religion, or an intellectual one, is disincarnate. If religion is doctrine, the life of the mind, then physical death has no place, and grief is at best a private act. In public one should appear to be stolid and secure. In the funeral chapels in our community there are "family rooms," where the most intimate mourners sit during the service. In most cases I cannot even see them, nor they me. But their private grief is protected. While it is true that most grief is a lonely, or at least a solitary, business or one which can only be expressed within the privacy of the family, there is grief which is appropriately shared with the community, particularly the church. The recovery of grief is part of the recovery of the passion which can lead us out of the dark prisons where we have been held.

Of the six memorial services held in the church, one was for my son who was killed in the crash of a private airplane. Hundreds of people from the congregation and the community gathered, and our family sat surrounded by those who shared our sorrow. Yes, I will remember John every time I enter the room. No, I was not brave or sturdy. And yes, my grief and theirs, was a healing, life-giving experience. It was not the only time I grieved before them. For the next few weeks no Sunday service passed without my having to stop somewhere in the midst of it and let the feelings and the tears do their cleansing work. But that congregation was my faith community. I put myself, my life, my broken heart in their hands, and I was not ashamed. They shared in my healing, both in the larger congregation and in the special ministry of the Ebb Tide Fellowship described in chapter four. The church was the community which celebrated the liberating work of Christ for and with me.

How can we expect the church to offer us liberation from the terrible bonds of isolation, privatism and meaninglessness by which we middle-class people are bound, if we refuse to allow our deepest feelings to be entrusted to the hands of the community of faith? The loneliness, ennui, and detachment we experience in the depths, as well as the heights, of life are not addressed, and we drag these terrible chains with us. But it need not be. God has promised to set us free, and the church celebrates by what it does as well as by what it believes—indeed what it believes flows from what it does—the liberating power of Christ. If liberation has meaning within the context of our congregations it must, at least, provide the following basic affirmations Moltmann has identified for us:

—that no one is alone with his or her problems,
—that no one has to conceal his or her disabilities,
—that there are not some who have the say and others who have nothing to say,
—that neither the old nor the little ones are isolated,

—that one hears the other even when it is unpleasant and there is no agreement, and
—that, finally, the one can also at times leave the other in peace when the other needs it.[3]

A congregation can also provide other avenues of liberation for those trapped in the captivities of an affluent culture. Consider the following circumstances:

Mary and John are considering giving up the middle-class life altogether and living on the land somewhere. They want to rear their children outside what they consider the corruption of public education, while they give full time to the peace movement. They are conflicted and hurt by the isolation they experience. What role can a liberating church play as they struggle with that decision?

Arthur is financially secure, but he is terribly unhappy. He desperately wants to break out of his old patterns and spend the rest of his life doing something "to serve human need." How does he go about seeking advice and support from the congregation?

Martha had gone through a long and difficult struggle over the custody of her children. Because of her well documented misconduct, the court agrees with her husband and awards him custody. She is grief-stricken. How does the congregation deal with her captivity? In what context can she ask for help?

After thirty years with the same company, Sam is fired. He has no pension, has not prepared for the eventuality and feels trapped by a situation over which he now has no control. Does a liberating church have anything to say or do about his turmoil?

One Sunday a man, who appears to have wandered in off the streets, finds himself in an upper middle-class congregation. His dress and manner mark him as quite different from the well groomed people around him. Because this is a *liberal* group, he is welcomed. He feels so good about his welcome he becomes an evangelist. Suddenly a half dozen, and then a score of persons like himself, who are from boarding homes or who live in halfway houses of a state hospital, are deeply involved in the church. They attend everything. Some of the men begin to ask the proper women of the church for dates. There is obvious discomfort. One such person was okay, but this influx is troublesome. Who is captive of what, and how does a congregation deal with various captivities?

A group of people in the congregation want to engage in a protest demonstration at nearby missile sites. They believe that as Christians they can no longer sit by and allow what they consider weapons of doom to go unchallenged by the Christian community. Many other members of the congregation draw their livelihoods from the military facility which supports the sites. What does a congregation concerned about liberation do?

Alene is an executive at a local plant under investigation for the improper storage of agricultural chemicals. This long-time practice has resulted in two suspected deaths among migrant laborers. The survival of the plants is necessary for the welfare of the economy of the community. Alene is a pillar of the church, and has been a "blessing to the congregation" for years. Now what?

In a community in which low-cost rental housing is scarce, Sylvester, an elder of the church, makes a modest living by owning and operating a series of slum houses. He buys them as cheaply as he can; milks them for a few years and abandons them. He now feels as if there is a conflict between how he has supported himself and what God would have him do. He wants to be set free from his captivity. How does he ask the church to help solve his problem?

These are just a few of the captivities people within our congregations face. None are fictional, although the circumstances have been altered to protect anonymity. Each situation brings with it its own devastating bondage, the kind of bondage which is

THE LIBERATING POWER OF PASSION 163

probably peculiar to middle-class people. These are not the captivities of the Third World, although there are commonalities. If we are to be set free by the power of the gospel, the people of God must be involved in God's liberating acts. I leave it to you to work your way through these or situations you know firsthand, and determine what liberation theology has to say about your *project* and *praxis*, which may not be such disincarnate and emotionless words at all!

As you struggle with these problems, keep in mind a few of the basic presuppositions upon which liberation theology rests:

—God has a preferential option for the poor.
—In the struggle between the oppressors and the oppressed, God always stands with the oppressed.
—The liberation of the oppressors depends on their being radically transformed—being born again, Jesus called it.
—Liberating action precedes doctrinal clarity.
—To know God is to do justice.
—The Messianic Age, and the kingdom which it announces, do not look like the kingdoms of this world.
—The project given to the church is not to bring in the kingdom, but to declare its coming and to demonstrate how life will be lived when it arrives in God's final liberating event.
—Compassion is the prelude to passion and the cross.
—Often new wineskins are necessary to carry the new wine.
—The oppressed are often too close to see.
—Liberation and liturgy are related.
—Egyptians always find themselves in a difficult position.
—The principalities and powers are persistent and very strong. Making friends with them is a deadly temptation.

Before we leave specific problems which involve congregations, and which have more to do with feelings and actions than points of view or classical theological constructs, we must deal with one other difficult matter, the explosion of charismatic religion in the First World. Fewer subjects have been more troublesome for many mainline churches. Congregations have been torn apart by a few charismatics, who infiltrate and split otherwise peaceful churches.

Charismatics I have run across often interpret ministry in the Third World only in terms of cultural displacement, conversion or perhaps charity. Rarely is it seen in terms of justice and freedom. The growth of the charismatic movement appears to many of us to be another evidence of the sectarian other-worldly way in which Christians have often avoided facing the implications of the gospel.

Having laid out that clear personal position, allow me to offer a very large *however*. It may be that the charismatic movement is a way God has chosen to chasten an otherwise emotionally and spiritually sterile church. What we may be experiencing is an appropriate response to our rationality. If nature seeks an equilibrium, we, having squeezed the body of Christ into the diver's helmet, may discover that the charismatic movement is a liberating word from the Lord. To put it in less sweeping terms, the emotional excesses of many of our brothers and sisters may be a corrective for our emotional sterility.

If so, it would not be the first time this has occurred. The Wesleys arrived on the scene with their heart-warming experiences at a time when the spirit of much of the established churches had dried up. Great waves of revivalism followed the captivity of the church by the precepts of the Enlightenment. Healing ministries have developed in an era when we seem to have committed ourselves totally to science as the remedy for all human ills. It is possible that the charismatic movement is one of God's living parables. "He who has ears to hear, let him hear."

The essence of the charismatic movement can be affirmed in another way, without getting bogged down in vagaries of how it is often embodied. Perhaps we can discover a more authentic expression of what the gifts of the Spirit are about. In our rejection of these phenomena we may have lost a critical element in the meaning of Christian faith and witness. To the contrary, we should affirm that God, through the work of the Holy Spirit, has given the church extraordinary gifts we ought to claim, celebrate and use to God's glory and human wholeness.

Perhaps the gift of tongues is not the ability to speak in some heavenly language, or irrational gibberish, whichever the case may be, but to speak in an earthly language which is so out of harmony with what is currently being said that those who hear think the speakers are filled with wine; even if it is only nine or eleven in the morning. In our society to speak with and for the oppressed in the Third World, or the oppressed too close to see, is often to use an unknown tongue. At times when I have known that through the Spirit of God I was proclaiming the liberating gospel of Christ, there have been listeners certain I had lost my senses. But the marginalized and oppressed in the congregation knew what I was saying, and heard it gladly. For an Egyptian to speak for the Hebrews, and in their own language—thought forms—must seem like an exotic and altogether dangerous utterance to the rest of the Egyptians. If our gift is the interpretation of tongues, it may be that the Holy Spirit has given some of us the capacity to explain to our First World brothers and sisters what the cries of the oppressed mean, and how we can respond.

Prophecy may be more than forth telling. It may be, in fact, foretelling: making it clear that if we continue to follow our present course with its exploitation, its reliance on institutionalized violence, its gutting of the world's economies and resources to produce and maintain a defense establishment whose purpose is to ensure that nothing changes, we are under the judgment of God. The wages of sin are death. The wages of our collective sins may be universal death.

The gift of healing may be exactly that. We have described it elsewhere in this book. As with these and the other gifts of the Spirit, the fundamental test is "Do they edify the church?" (1 Corinthians 14:4). The charismata are real gifts for a real church. If they have been twisted and used in ways which neither edify the church nor proclaim the liberation Christ came to bring, then we need to redeem them from sectarian heresy, just as Paul attempted to do so among the Corinthians (1 Corinthians 12-14).

If we are to be saved from our captivities, we might be advised not to assume too quickly when or in what ways God will choose or has chosen to liberate us. "The Son of Man will come when you least expect him."

Notes

1. Jurgen Moltmann, *The Open Church*, Fortress Press, 1978, pp. 23-4.
2. *Ibid.* pp. 64-5.
3. *Ibid.* p. 33.

11

God's Final Victory

Liberation theology is rooted in eschatology—God's final victory. Our battles with the principalities and powers are not futile efforts to hold back the tide. The ultimate trust is in the One to whom the ultimate victory belongs. It is not simply a political *modus vivendi*, or a way to use the folk religion of a culture to accomplish a social agenda. While it is true that there is no shortage of examples from the history of the church in which political figures have sought ways to co-opt the religious institution, we find insubstantial evidence to tag Latin American liberationists with that brush.

Certainly the major theological figures have first of all derived their perspectives from the Bible. They are not politicians who have found the church a ready ally. They are men and women who see liberation as the will of God and believe that the problems of the oppressed call for a political solution. Moltmann argues that the effort has not been to politicize Christianity, but to Christianize politics.

Nor is the goal of liberationism to establish the kingdom of God, make it a reality on earth as it is in heaven. This is God's ultimate work. Our work is the proximate task of being faithful to the project we have been given. We do not trust in our capacity to manufacture a perfect society, but in the God who has given us a clearly defined task, which is a mile marker on the way to the kingdom. Our faith resides in the God who has acted, is acting and will finally act to establish the sovereign rule we call God's kingdom. Although many liberationists hold that the kingdom will come within history, most draw a clear distinction between the church's project and the consummation of God's sovereign reign. Marx's classless society and the kingdom of God are not to be confused, even though among some theologians they are closely linked. Leonard Boff quotes Paul VI who held:

> The church links human liberation and salvation in Jesus Christ, but she never identifies them, because she knows through revelation, historical experiences and the reflection of faith that not every notion of liberation is necessarily consistent and compatible with an evangelical vision of man, of things and of events.[1]

It was this same Pope who argued in the Encyclical *Evangelii Nutiandi*:

> The church ... has the duty to proclaim the liberation of millions of human beings, many of whom are her own children.... This is not foreign to evangelization. ... the church is certainly not willing to restrict her mission only to the religious field and dissociate herself from man's temporal problems.[2]

Liberation, according to the bishops who met at Puebla in 1979, goes far beyond the temporal realm, and should not be identified with any human institutional structure:

> Our people yearn for a full and integral liberation, not one confined to the realm of temporal existence. It extends beyond that to a full communion with God and with one's brothers and sisters in eternity. And that communion is already beginning to be realized, however imperfectly.[3]

These statements hardly lead to an otherworldly metaphysical system which gives Christians permission to ignore the realities of oppression and despair here and now. There is no hint anywhere of "integral liberation," being construed to mean be patient if you have nothing in this life, because finally God will act and you will have your reward in the next. That always has been and still is heresy, be it proclaimed by ecclesiatical narcotics peddlers among the oppressed, or by comfortable hucksters who salve the consciences of the affluent. In either case it is a denial of the incarnation. As Gutierrez says:

> Hope of the resurrection is in no sense an evasion of concrete history; on the contrary, it leads to a redoubling of effort in the struggle against what brings unjust death.... Belief in the resurrection is incompatible with the acceptance of a society that condemns the poor to death. To be aware of this, and to act accordingly, is a central aspect of being "witnesses to Easter."[4]

In the basic source book from which much of liberation theology has been derived, Gutierrez puts it this way:

> To assert that faith and political action have nothing to say to each other is to imply that they move on juxtaposed and unrelated planes. If one accepts this assertion, either he will have to engage in verbal gymnastics to show—without succeeding—how faith should express itself in a commitment to a more just society; or the result is that faith comes to coexist, in a most opportunistic manner, with any political option.[5]

Liberationism sees what the kingdom is like—basically from the biblical sources—and moves toward it. The church is a beachhead of the kingdom. It is really more than a roadsign. It is rather a penetration of the future into the present. It is a reality which is not yet here and which will arrive fully by God's act, but which can be demonstrated here and now. We have been given the task of providing evidences of its reality in our own time and place. These evidences are more than a teaser, a preview of coming attractions. To experience them is to see what God finally and fully wills for us, and for all. Liberationism reaches into the future, brings back chunks of it and says: "Here, here is what the kingdom is like!" Is not this what Jesus did? Boff makes the point when he holds:

> Liberation is the act of gradually delivering reality from the various captivities to which it is historically subject and which run counter to God's historic project—which is the upbuilding of the kingdom, a kingdom in which everything is orientated to God, penetrated by God's presence and glorified, on the cosmic level as on the personal level.... Liberation shows forth the activity of eschatological salvation by antici-

pation, as the leaven of today is the dough of a reality to be transfigured in the eschaton.[6]

Obviously great care must be taken lest we become triumphalistic, believing we can describe God's kingdom in its fullness by pointing to any current political system or even a utopian social dream. The greatest temptation and the most demonic risk inherent in liberation thought is to believe the kingdom of God is nothing more than an eschatological extension of our political agendas.

Franz Liszt wrote a beautiful, if seldom performed, oratorio called *The Legend of St. Elizabeth*, in which the tempter's apple is swallowed whole. It is the story of a twelfth century Slovokian Princess, who was married off, for political reasons, to a foreign Duke. Being a good Christian, she had great compassion for the poor, and would travel the land giving bread to the most destitute of the realm. But it was the Duke's bread, and he, not being a Christian, took a dim view of this redistribution of his wealth. He forbade her to continue her charitable activities, but she persisted without his knowledge. One day he caught her red-handed on the path to the cottage of a woodcutter's poor family. He tore the basket from her hands, but discovered that it was filled with roses, not bread.

The basket had contained bread when she started out that morning, but in order to protect Elizabeth from the wrath of her husband, an angel had performed a miracle, thus the roses. Being truly pious, Elizabeth confessed that she had really been taking bread to the poor against her husband's wishes, despite the appearance of flowers. She also insisted that it was God's work she was about, and that she intended to continue performing her acts of charity no matter what he, the Duke, said, and despite the angel's attempt to rescue her.

The Duke was so struck by her faith he was converted on the spot. To put it in modern terms, he took Christ as his personal Savior and committed himself to follow the Lord and to perform works of righteousness for Jesus' sake. He returned home, mobilized all the men in his domain and charged off in full military regalia to kill as many Turks as he could lay his sword on. As the militia marched to the gory encounter, the Crusaders sang about the mission to which God had called them. The melody still appears in most modern hymn books, and is one of our all time favorites. The tune is either listed as "St. Elizabeth's" or "The Crusaders Hymn." Fortunately we have altered the words, and now know it as "Fairest Lord Jesus."

The Duke obviously assumed that the policies of the nation coincided with the voice of God. He and thousands of others, who journeyed to the Holy Land on similar missions, had heard Urban II cry out, "Gott wult!" The risk is that in whatever age and from whatever perspective we tend to confuse a political agenda, dressed up in religious garb, with the voice and the will of God. As right-wing causes have often gotten trapped, we have no reason to doubt that it can also happen to left-wing causes. Once liberationism assumes it is called to determine and actualize in history the perfect will of God, it is in serious trouble.

Just as the Duke got it wrong, just as nationalists, sectarians and fundamentalists have usually gotten it wrong, the risk is that we, too, might get it wrong. Fortunately we have a clear and identifiable description of what God's kingdom is like; a model against which we can lay any political movement. We discover it, as we have insisted throughout this study, in almost every section of the Bible. The agenda appears in bold relief once we see God as the One who stands with the oppressed. For Christians it is adequately described in the Sermon on the Mount, and in the kingdom parables of Jesus. It is displayed in his mighty works, which are outcroppings of what God is ready to do. John the Baptist declared that the kingdom of God was at hand, and Jesus produced evidences of its reality.

We are not making a blind guess. We know, by the evidence, what the kingdom yet to come will be like. Even if we have only an outline, it is clear enough so that we can act with integrity. Ours is more than a leap of faith. It is a leap based on evidence assuring us, to the extent faith is assurance, that we shall land safely even if we cannot see the exact spot of the landing. We act in light of the clear biblical record. As Langdon Gilkey says: "The major theme of both Testaments is the coming of new possibilities into human life, the freeing from bondage of freedom and of fate, and in the end from the bondage of death."[7]

GOD'S FINAL VICTORY   171

Hugo Echegaray describes what liberationists see as inseparable messages running through the life and teachings of Jesus:

> There are two main themes that give the message of Jesus its structure: the imminent coming of God's reign and the radical call of God to conversion and acceptance of the dynamics of the kingdom. On the one hand, then, there is the kingdom as an eschatological . . . gift of salvation, freely offered by God without dependence on our efforts to obtain it. On the other hand, there is the urgent call to begin moving toward the kingdom and to prepare for it by the effort to transform our history, an effort that the kingdom itself at one and the same time stimulates, promises, and presupposes—on the one hand, the future form of the kingdom; on the other hand, its present form.[8]

Gilkey who sees the biblical notion of the kingdom as an extension of the life of Jesus as well as a sociological reality, puts it this way:

> The kingdom represents, therefore, the perfected social community that corresponds to the personal and individual perfection of the figure of Jesus, a perfection then realized only in him. The symbol of the kingdom thus functions in relation to ongoing historical and political life as the individual perfection of Jesus as the Christ functions in relation to the crises, despair and fragmentary realizations of individual Christian existence. It establishes the ultimate norms, the final bases for critical judgment, for positive policies, and for political and communal action, much as the individual perfection of Jesus' life set the ultimate norms for our own fragmentary good works.

Gilkey goes on to argue that both of these counsels of perfection are, in the final analysis, eschatological.

> Both the complete sanctification of our individual existence and that of communal existence remain eschatological hopes; in both areas our experience is of fragmentary fulfillment at best, and in both we

remain dependent in the end on the forgiveness and
the promise of God for ultimate fulfillment.[9]

So the Christian lives in anticipation of the kingdom that has not yet appeared, but works as if it were already in our midst. We live in anticipation. But anticipation is not wish dreaming. Anticipation is to act now as if it were already the future. It is to live a step ahead of the now. It is to celebrate as present what is yet to be. As Jurgen Moltmann says: "It is a payment made in advance of complete fulfillment, and part possession of what is still to come."[10]

What gives anyone the audacity to live that way? How is it we find courage to occupy God's not yet as if it were a present reality? We know that the world does not now bear the configuration of the reign of God. Yet we are called to live kingdom lives in a land we have yet to see. As with Abraham and Sarah, it is a land of promise, a land we seek as an inheritance, a land to which we go not even knowing we are going.

At the base of liberation theology lies a trust in the ultimate triumph of God. The Christian hope, which is simply the extension of faith into the future, as love is the action of faith in the present, rests on God's mighty acts. As God stood at the beginning of history as its creator, stands in the midst of history as its sustainer, so God will stand at the end of history as its consummator, liberator and victor. Beyond the pious hope that someday God will win the final victory, we live in the conviction that the victory has already been accomplished in the resurrection of Christ. If we reach into the future and bring back a chunk of it into the present, through the proclamation of the resurrection of Christ, we bear witness in our own time and place that even the last enemy has been overcome by the power of God.

In chapter six we talked about the principalities and powers as a shorthand way to describe those forces over which we have no control. What in Paul's days were astrological authorities and dominions, are in our day political and technological systems. The Christian hope affirms that even though they still seem to be in charge, the war is over and God has emerged victorious. All that awaits is the final sentence. The wheat and the tares have grown together, and the tares have not yet been plucked out. The

Lord of the harvest has already declared what their fate shall be. "One little word shall fell them." That word has been pronounced. God has already won the victory. It is in that hope we reach into the future and live now as if the kingdom has already come.

We no longer need to be taken in by those who are bound to the deceits of this age, to the philosophy that might is the only arbiter of the human condition, or that "the only thing *they* understand is brute force!" or that "there can never be a just society. After all, didn't Jesus say 'the poor you will have with you always'?" Yet the temptation exists to live faithlessly, as if the victory of Christ had not been won.

In an Easter sermon, David Jenkins, the Bishop of Durham, raised a considerable theological fracas in Britain when he suggested that the Christian faith does not rest on the belief that Jesus' physical body left the tomb. "Heresy! Faithlessness! Paganism!" were cries heard around the land. Liberation theology affirms that to be heretical, faithless and pagan is not to question whether Jesus did or did not physically come forth from the tomb, but to deny by the way we live that God has won the victory over death. It is not that we hold a faulty doctrine, but that we do not act in light of the resurrection. Liberationists affirm that living the victory of the resurrection must precede accepting it as an article of faith.

> See to it that no one makes a prey of you by philosophy and empty deceits, according to human tradition, according to the elemental spirits of the universe, and not according to Christ. (Colossians 2:8).

We are no longer captives of these elemental spirits, these principalities and powers, the rulers of this present generation. We have been made alive in Christ. We live in the actualized hope of the resurrection. We have been bonded into Christ's living body, the church. We have shared in his death and been raised in his likeness. We are no longer under the dominion of sin. We are sons and daughters who are already forgiven, called to wholeness, liberated from our sins and their consequences.

> You were buried with him in baptism, in which you were also raised with him through faith in the working

of God, who raised him from the dead. And you, who were dead in trespasses and the uncircumcision of your flesh, God made alive together with him, having forgiven us all our trespasses, having cancelled the bond which stood against us with its legal demands; this he set aside, nailing it to the cross (Colossians 2:12-14).

But what of the principalities and powers which still seem to rule this age? "He disarmed the principalities and powers and made a public example of them, triumphing over them in him" (Colossians 2:15). They have been defeated! Here is the ultimate good news of the gospel! The principalities and powers have been rendered harmless. They have no authority any more. Through the cross, God has established a new order. A new creation has come to birth, populated by those who share in the new creation. The era of the kingdom has already dawned. God's ultimate disarmament program is already in place. Note the active verb. It is not that God pleaded with, convinced, cajoled, appeased the principalities and powers so that they saw the wisdom of laying down their weapons. God did not initiate a petition drive, engage in demonstrations or do any of the other things appropriate to our project. God didn't conduct an educational effort; they were simply stripped of their authority. God has taken the weapons out of their hands. Or to put it in contemporary terms God has unilaterally declared that the kingdom is to be a nuclear-free zone; a place where oppression, captivity, marginalization of any kind no longer have any authority, nor even the right to exist.

The Christian proclamation, the preaching of the good news, consists in this: that in the name of Christ and by the power of the cross those things which have formerly held power over the lives of people are defeated. God has established sovereignty over the cosmic enemies. They are helpless. They have been disarmed. The chains of our captivities have been cut away. We no longer need to cooperate with the principalities and powers as if they were still in command. We stand as victors against those demonic forces.

We cry out: "In the name of Christ, the Lord: no more!" We do not need to stumble over our words, trying to explain why we

GOD'S FINAL VICTORY   175

yet appear to be under the control of economic and political forces which oppress and dismantle the hopes of masses of God's children. We live and work as if God's kingdom were fully present regardless of the spasms and death throes of the old order. Every Christian congregation is called to proclaim the victory God has already won. We refuse to pay lip service to, duty to, bow before gods which have been defeated. If we are still in their world, we are no longer of their world. Indeed, it is not their world any more! The age of despair and oppression is passing away.

Our project consists in celebrating ways in which the new creation is coming among us. And if the old regimes still seem to be in control, we know God's truth is sure. No matter how peculiar the "real world" thinks us to be, we have been let in on the end of the story, and we live as if that end were already accomplished among us. It is not secret knowledge, or a private story, except as we fail to share it. As Christian congregations our project is, by God's grace, to be a people who no longer cooperate with the demonic, because we know the demonic has no power. We are that community faithful to the one whose cross has redeemed the world. We live under the sovereignty of God.

If there is any place today where it might seem there has been no victory, no defeat of the principalities and powers, no dawning of the age of the kingdom, no act of God, it is among the black population in South Africa. At the funeral of one of his thin line of co-workers in the cause of liberation, Bishop Desmond Tutu closed the occasion with a quotation from the book of Revelation. It is a passage he often uses as an expression of the Christian hope and the ultimate victory of God. We end this guide to liberation theology for middle-class congregations with the same thundering affirmation.

> After this I looked and saw a vast throng, which no one could count, from every nation, of all tribes, peoples and languages, standing in front of the throne and before the Lamb. They were robed in white and had palms in their hands, and they shouted together: "Victory to our God who sits on the throne, and to the Lamb!" And all the angels stood round the throne and the elders and the four living creatures, and they fell

on their faces before the throne and worshipped God crying, "Amen! Praise and glory and wisdom, thanksgiving and honor, power and might, be to our God for ever and ever. Amen" (Revelation 7:9-12)[11]

Notes

1. Boff, *Salvation*, pp. 21-2.
2. *Ibid.* p. 21.
3. Latin American Bishops, "Puebla Document: Sec. 141."
4. Gutierrez, *We Drink*. p. 118.
5. Gutierrez, *A Theology*. p. 236.
6. Boff, *Salvation*. p. 57.
7. Gilkey, *Challenge*. p. 123.
8. Echegaray, *The Practice of Jesus*. pp. 79-80.
9. Gilkey, *Challenge*. pp. 125-6.
10. Jurgen Moltmann, *The Church in the Power of the Spirit*, SCM Press, 1977, p. 193.
11. "From *The New English Bible*, 1976. The delegates of the Oxford University Press, Inc., and The Syndics of the Cambridge University Press, 1961, 1970. Reprinted by permission.")

www.ingramcontent.com/pod-product-compliance
Lightning Source LLC
Chambersburg PA
CBHW051933160426
43198CB00012B/2135